To

David

From

Leonard Lo

Happy Christmas
2006

Enjoy the eating !!.

The Opera House Cookbook

THE
OPERA HOUSE
COOKBOOK

Compiled by Robin Hambro

With a Foreword by Sir Geraint Evans

Illustrated by Simon Gooch

Weidenfeld and Nicolson
London

First published in Great Britain by
George Weidenfeld and Nicolson Ltd
91 Clapham High Street, London SW4 7TA

Copyright © Robin Hambro 1980
Illustrations copyright © Simon Gooch 1980

ISBN 0 297 77806 4

Set, printed and bound in Great Britain by
Fakenham Press Limited, Fakenham, Norfolk

Contents

Foreword

Good food has always been associated with opera stars and conductors. *The Opera House Cookbook* confirms this fact. The recipes are beloved favourites of internationally famous singers and conductors and are used by them in their personal entertaining. This collection of recipes shows a richness of life and an appreciation of good food, which comes not only from a deep artistic commitment to opera and music but to life in general. I hope that you will enjoy this glimpse into the personal life of the opera world and these unusual and varied recipes.

Geraint Evans.

Introduction

It has been said that cook books make enjoyable reading; and *The Opera House Cookbook* will give more pleasure than most. It combines a selection of recipes, some inventive and original, and some old favourites with an added individual artistic approach. It also includes brief profiles of the contributors, all of whom are internationally famous opera stars and conductors who obviously devote a great deal of time and thought to food.

The proceeds of this book will go to the Royal Opera House Trust, a registered charity, which supports the work of The Royal Opera House by providing funds for new productions and for the maintenance of its high standards.

The recipes have been tried and tested and for the most part are easy to follow and take little time to prepare. If there are any in the book which resemble existing recipes already attributed to other sources, I would like to apologize in advance.

The production of this book would never have been possible had I not been part of The Royal Opera House. The enthusiasm of all the contributors is gratefully acknowledged. My thanks also to Lord Weidenfeld, Kate Dunning and Linda Osband of Weidenfeld and Nicolson, Sir Geraint Evans, Arthur Hammond, Vicki Cliff Hodges, Maria Grazia de la Garda, Norton, Rose, Botterell and Roche, Jennie Selby, Caroline Rennie, Donald Southern and Katharine Wilkinson, all of whom helped in various ways. My greatest thanks go to Sue Foll without whose hard work and untiring enthusiasm this book would not have been possible.

Robin Hambro
Royal Opera House Trust,
45 Floral Street,
London, WC2

The artists' recordings are not mentioned as they are all extensive and not all of their operatic roles can be included.

Measuring and Weighing Notes

Due to the variety of recipes which are for the most part presented in their original form, this chart might be of some help.

Imperial Measures	Approximate Metric Equivalents
ounces	grams
1	25
2	50
3	75
4	100–125
5	150
6	175
7	200
8	225–250
9	250
10	275
11	300
12	350–375
14	400
15	425
16 = 1 lb	450
17	475
18	500
19	550
20 = 1¼ lbs	575
1½ lbs	700
2 lbs	1000 = 1 kg
2½ lbs	1.1 kg
3 lbs	1.5 kg

United Kingdom Standard Metric Pack   500 grams = 1 lb

Oven Temperatures

	C	F	Gas Mark
Very cool	110	225	$\frac{1}{4}$
Cool, low	140	275	1
Moderate	160	325	3
Medium hot	190	375	5
Hot	220	425	7
Very hot	240	475	9

Spoon Measures

All spoon measures used in this book are level unless otherwise stated. Please remember that the Australian tablespoon holds 20 ml, the American tablespoon holds 14.2 ml and the British tablespoon 17.7 ml.

The teaspoon of all countries is the same, approx 5 ml.

Imperial–North American Solid Measure Guide

Imperial	North American
1 lb flour	4 cups
1 lb butter	2 cups
1 lb granulated sugar	2 cups
1 lb icing sugar	3 cups

Liquid Measures

Imperial Measures (ounces)	Approximate Metric Equivalents
1 fluid ounce	25 ml
2 fluid ounces	50 ml
3 ,,	75 ml
4 ,,	100 ml
5 ,,	150 ml
6 ,,	175 ml
7 ,,	200 ml
8 ,,	225 ml
9 ,,	250 ml
10 ,,/$\frac{1}{2}$ pint	300 ml or 1$\frac{1}{4}$ cups liquid USA
20 ,,/1 pint	600 ml or 2$\frac{1}{2}$ cups USA
1$\frac{1}{2}$ pints/1 litre	1000 ml or 3$\frac{3}{4}$ cups USA

Please note that the British Imperial pint = 20 fl oz
while the American pint = 16 fl oz

Starters

Berit Lindholm

This dramatic Swedish soprano, who is a member of the Stockholm Opera, has appeared in many famous opera houses throughout the world. She specializes in Wagnerian roles such as Brünnhilde and Isolde. Her other roles include Cassandra, Leonore and Turandot.

Hot-baked Matjessil (Hot-baked Herrings)

FOR 1–2 PEOPLE

herrings (*matjes*)
butter
1 hard-boiled egg (minced)
leeks or onions
parsley and/or dill

Put each *matjesfilet* on foil, add some butter, the minced hard-boiled egg, a leek or onion in rings and the parsley and/or dill. Fold up the foil into parcels and bake them in a hot oven for 10–15 minutes.

Serve the filets with boiled potatoes.

'I like a glass of beer and a piece of crisp hard rye bread and butter with *matjesfilet*. If you can have a nap afterwards, why not treat yourself to a Scandinavian "Snaps" like Aalborg as well. *Bon appetit*.'

Lawrence Foster

He has appeared as guest conductor with most major North
American and European orchestras and is currently principal
conductor and music director of the Houston Symphony. His
wide repertoire includes most classical works as well as
twentieth-century music. He has recently conducted *Così fan tutte*
and a new production of *Troilus and Cressida*.

Eggplant with Scordolea

FOR 6 PEOPLE

3 eggplants (aubergines)
100–150 gm oil
500 gm potatoes (the kind used for mashed potatoes)
20 walnuts
10 cloves of garlic
salt, pepper, vinegar
1 kg tomatoes
1 bunch parsley
100 gm olives

Cut the eggplants into slices thick as a finger and sprinkle salt on
to both sides. Put them under a wooden board with a weight on
top to let the bitter juice drain out. Dry them with kitchen paper
and fry them in heated oil. When ready, arrange eggplants on
the bottom of a pan, one next to the other (do not discard the
used oil). Separately, boil the potatoes and mash them well.
Then mix them gradually with 5–6 spoons of oil using a
wooden spoon. Add shredded walnuts, cloves of garlic well
pressed, salt, pepper and vinegar as desired. This mixture is
called *Scordolea*. Spread it on to the eggplant slices. Boil and peel
the tomatoes, cut them into small pieces, and put them into the
same pan with the oil used to fry the eggplant until the sauce
thickens. Add chopped parsley, a little salt and spread the
tomato sauce over the *Scordolea*. Decorate each slice of eggplant
with a few olives.

Renato Bruson

This Italian baritone is well known for his interpretations of Donizetti and Verdi. He has sung in the major opera houses of North America, Europe and Great Britain. His many roles include Ankarström in *Un Ballo in Maschera*, Rodrigo, Renato, Miller in *Luisa Miller* and Alfonso.

Timbale di Riso (Rice Mould)

FOR 4−5 PEOPLE

1 small onion	1 clove of garlic
stock	parsley
40 gm unsalted butter	50 gm Parmesan
500 gm rice	3 eggs
350 gm fresh mushrooms	breadcrumbs
oil	salt

Prepare a risotto with chopped onion, stock, butter and rice. Clean and slice mushrooms, fry with oil, garlic and parsley and put aside.

When risotto is ready add Parmesan. Allow to cool. When cold add 2 of the eggs, beaten, and form the rice mixture into balls. Then make a cavity in each ball so that they look like shells or baskets. Roll these in the remaining beaten egg, then in breadcrumbs, and fry in very hot oil. When they are firm and cooked, fill with mushrooms or any other vegetable mixture and season to taste.

Anne Pashley

A British-born soprano who started her career as a sprinter in the Olympics before changing to opera. She has sung with all the British companies and has been heard in the roles of Idamante, Nancy, Cherubino, Amor and Zerlina. She is noted for her fine acting abilities.

Spaghetti al Pesto

FOR 4 PEOPLE

In early summer buy or grow a basil plant as you will have trouble getting fresh leaves. Cut off $1\frac{1}{2}$ cups of leaves. Pulverize them with

	$\frac{1}{4}$ cup pine nut kernels
	$\frac{3}{4}$ cup grated Parmesan cheese
blend in	$\frac{3}{4}$ cup olive oil
	2 cloves garlic

Pour over 1 lb cooked spaghetti and mix up. Put in a hot oven for a few minutes in an oven-proof dish and serve.

This is also a marvellous spread on large baked potatoes.

Peter Maag

The Swiss conductor known for his knowledge and interpretations of Mozart operas. His range of opera is wide and also includes operetta. He appears throughout the world in opera houses and concert halls. Being artistic director of the Turin Opera is the latest post in his career.

Spaghetti alla Sarda (Sardinian Spaghetti)

FOR 4–6 PEOPLE

1 teacup dry raisins
3 teaspoons olive oil
½ teacup pinoli (pine seed)
½ teacup salted capers
½ teacup black olives, cut in half
6 anchovy fillets cut in pieces
1 can sardines in oil, drained and chopped
some juniper berries
150 gm spaghetti
salt

In a mixing bowl put dry raisins, 2 teaspoons olive oil, pine seeds, capers, olives, anchovies, sardines and juniper berries. Cook spaghetti in salted water, stirring from time to time. When cooked *al dente*, add the spaghetti to the sauce. Heat up in a frying pan for several minutes, then serve very hot.

Anne Pashley

Humus

FOR 2–4 PEOPLE

½lb chick peas
1 dessertspoon sesame paste
2 dessertspoons sunflower or olive oil
2 cloves garlic
½ cup lemon juice
parsley

Soak the chick peas overnight and cook until soft, or pressure cook, unsoaked, for about an hour. Cool. Put these together with the sesame paste, oil, garlic and lemon juice into a liquidizer with some of the water from the boiled peas. Blend to a smooth paste, adding more of the water if necessary. Serve in a flattish dish and garnish with a little more oil and the chopped parsley. Chill. It is lovely spooned up with pieces of warm pitta bread.

You can vary the above ingredients to your taste.

Joan Sutherland

Australia's great *prima donna* has performed on every major stage in the world. Amongst her many roles are Violetta, Maria Stuarda, Lucia di Lammermoor, Norma and Lucrezia Borgia. She is now particularly renowned for nineteenth-century *bel canto* roles by Rossini, Donizetti and Bellini and has made recordings of most of her famous roles. She has appeared with every major opera house in the world and was made a Dame Commander of the British Empire for her services to music. Her husband, Richard Bonynge, now conducts most of her performances.

Mushrooms à la Grecque

FOR 6 PEOPLE

1 finely chopped onion
4 tablespoons olive oil
¼ pint dry white wine
bouquet garni

1 clove of garlic, crushed
salt and pepper
½ lb tomatoes, skinned (or 1 can)
1 lb button mushrooms
chopped parsley

Sauté onion in half the oil until soft. Add wine, *bouquet garni*, garlic, salt and pepper, tomatoes and mushrooms, and cook gently for 10 minutes. Remove from heat and allow to cool. Add remainder of oil and chill. Serve cold as an appetizer, sprinkled with chopped parsley.

Forbes Robinson

A character English bass and a member of The Royal Opera for many years. He has sung with the Company abroad, in Europe and the Far East. His frequent guest appearances have taken him to many European and North and South American companies. Of his seventy roles he is most noted for Figaro, Boris Godunov and Don Basilio. The title role in *King Priam* was created by him and he was the first British artist to sing the role of Don Giovanni for the past hundred years.

Avocados Créole

Halve your avocados and fill with prawns, chopped stem ginger and pineapple. Top the lot with Thousand Island dressing. Serve with lightly buttered brown bread and nicely chilled Muscadet.

Renata Scotto

This attractive Italian soprano appears frequently at La Scala, Milan, and throughout the world. Now a resident of New York, where she has had many triumphs at the Metropolitan Opera, she has a large Italian repertoire particularly of Verdi, Puccini, Bellini and Donizetti. All her roles can now be heard on record.

Mozzarella in Carrozza

FOR 6–9 PEOPLE

2 12 oz Mozzarella balls
2 eggs
½ pint milk
salt
white pepper
1 family size loaf American bread (18 slices)
8 oz plain breadcrumbs
1 pint oil
4 oz butter
1 small onion
1 large tin tomatoes (preferably Del Monte)

Slice Mozzarella into ¼ inch slices. Beat the eggs and add some milk, salt and white pepper. Cut each slice of bread in half, dunk into the mixture and coat with breadcrumbs. Sandwich the Mozzarella slices between the slices of bread.

Heat the oil and butter in a frying pan and lower the heat once oil is hot. Fry the sandwiches on both sides until golden brown. To remove excess oil lay the sandwiches in a dish lined with paper kitchen towels, making sure that the Mozzarella doesn't stick to them. Remove to a serving dish and cover with tomato sauce, which can also be served separately.

To make the tomato sauce, thinly slice the onion and fry in a saucepan with the tomatoes and seasoning. Heat the whole until water has evaporated a little. The sauce is now ready to serve.

Cesare Siepi

This distinguished Italian bass is particularly remembered for his performances in the 1960s of Boris Godunov, Philip II, and many Verdi roles. He has spent much of his career with the Metropolitan Opera, New York, and La Scala, Milan. He is also famous in Vienna, at the Salzburg Festival and at Covent Garden, London, for his interpretation of the role of Don Giovanni. He often worked with the renowned conductors Toscanini, Furtwängler and Di Sabata.

Soufflé Suissesse

FOR 6 PEOPLE

4 oz butter
2½ oz flour
1 pint milk
4 egg yolks
5 egg whites
¾ pint cream
½ oz Parmesan ⎫
¼ oz Gruyere ⎬ grated finely
1 oz Cheddar ⎭
salt
pepper

First make a roux with the butter and flour. Add milk and bring to the boil. Add egg yolks and bring back to the boil for 2 minutes while whisking firmly. Whip the egg whites very firmly, then fold into the mixture. Have 12 tartelette moulds well buttered, and pour the mixture equally into the moulds. Place in a hot oven (450 °F) for 4 minutes.

Have a separate dish 1½ inches deep ×15–18 inches long. After the 4 minutes, take the soufflés from the oven and empty gently, one by one, into the spare dish. Put cream on top and then the cheese and seasoning. Replace quickly into the oven for 7–10 minutes, allowing them to rise and absorb the cream.

This soufflé was created for him by Michel and Albert Roux of Le Gavroche Restaurant, London.

25

Placido Domingo

An internationally-renowned Spanish tenor of great artistry and
musicianship, whose memorable voice was nurtured by his
Zarzuela (a type of Spanish operetta) singing parents. His
immense talent has been heard in all major opera houses of the
world in such roles as Cavaradossi, Don José, Otello, Rodolfo,
Manon Lescaut, Werther and many others. His repertoire is
probably larger than that of any other tenor and he ranks as the
most recorded opera star of today. He is also a talented
conductor and has appeared on the podium with the New York
City Opera, and in the opera houses of Munich, Hamburg and
San Francisco.

Epinard Pêcheur Domingo

FOR 2 PEOPLE

2 herrings, marinated	1 soupspoon creamed horseradish
2 lb fresh creamed spinach	½ lemon
1 small very finely chopped onion	black pepper

Marinate the raw herrings for at least 48 hours in oil and vinegar flavoured with chopped onions and peppercorns, then drain and cut into very small pieces.

Cream the rest of the ingredients together and fold in the fish.

This recipe was created by the Hill House Restaurant in Hampstead, London, in honour of Placido Domingo.

Isobel Buchanan

This young Scottish soprano made her debut in 1974 and attracted much attention. Already she has appeared at Glyndebourne, Covent Garden, the Vienna State Opera and Australian Opera, in such roles as Blanche (*Les Dialogues des Carmélites*), Pamina, Micaëla (*Carmen*) and Sophie (*Werther*).

Prawn Pâté

FOR 4 PEOPLE

250 gm prawns
45 gm butter
60 gm cream cheese
1 tablespoon mayonnaise
few drops Tabasco
good pinch nutmeg
1 small clove crushed garlic
2 teaspoons lemon juice

Shell and devein prawns and chop very finely. Mash the butter and cheese until soft. Add the seasonings, tasting as you go. Mix the ingredients together and pack into a small mould or dish. Serve with buttered toast or French bread. The dish improves by being made 6 hours before serving. Provided the prawns are fresh, the pâté will keep in the fridge for several days.

Maurits Sillem

This Swiss-born conductor of Dutch origin has lived in London for many years. He has worked with Glyndebourne Festival Opera, International Ballet Company, Sadler's Wells Opera, and is now Resident Conductor with The Royal Opera. He has recently conducted *Parsifal, Salome, Jenůfa, The Rake's Progress,* and given the English première of Peter Maxwell Davies' children's opera *The Two Fiddlers.*

Crab Mousse

FOR 4 PEOPLE

1 lb crab meat
1 tablespoon gelatine
3 tablespoons warm water
3 tablespoons warm cream
1 teaspoon each minced parsley, chives and green pepper
1 tablespoon each tomato chutney and lemon juice
½ pint cream, whipped

Dissolve gelatine by soaking in 3 tablespoons warm water and mix with the warm cream. Combine with all other ingredients. As the mixture thickens, fold in stiff whipped cream and pour into a mould. Cool until set, remove from the mould and serve with a sauce of equal parts mayonnaise (see below) and sour cream.

MAYONNAISE

Break 2 egg yolks at room temperature into a warm bowl with ¼ teaspoon salt. Add ½ pint fine olive oil, drop by drop at first. When it starts to thicken, beat constantly. When completely thick, add ½ teaspoon lemon juice and white pepper or mustard to taste.

Francis Egerton

A member of The Royal Opera, London, for many years, this tenor was born in Ireland and is known for his ability in roles both character and comic. Iopas, Pang in *Turandot*, Nick in *La fanciulla del West*, and Mime are among them. He has sung with all the British opera companies and many abroad.

Melon Salad and Herb Loaf

FOR 2–4 PEOPLE

1 Honeydew melon
1 lb tomatoes
1 large cucumber
salt
1 level tablespoon parsley,
    chopped
1 heaped teaspoon mint and
    chives, chopped

FRENCH DRESSING

2 level tablespoons wine vinegar
salt and pepper
1 tablespoon caster sugar
6 tablespoons salad oil

Remove seeds of melon and scoop out flesh in cubes. Skin and quarter the tomatoes. Squeeze out seeds and remove core. Cut again if large. Peel the cucumber and cube. Sprinkle cucumber with salt, cover with a plate and stand for 30 minutes. Drain and rinse cubes in cold water. Mix fruit and vegetables and pour over the dressing. Cover and chill 2–3 hours. Just before serving mix in the herbs.

HERB LOAF

4 oz butter
1 level tablespoon mixed
    dried herbs
juice ¼ lemon

black pepper
little crushed garlic (optional)
1 French loaf

Cream butter and herbs, lemon juice and seasoning. Add garlic if liked. Slice loaf ½ inch thick. Spread with mixture. Reshape loaf. Wrap in foil. Heat for 10 minutes at Gas Mark 7. Reduce for 5–8 minutes to Mark 6 unwrapped.

29

Tito Gobbi

The distinguished Italian baritone whose voice, intelligence and acting have made him renowned throughout the world. His fine interpretations of Puccini and Verdi characters are celebrated, particularly the roles of Falstaff and Iago. His operatic repertoire covered over a hundred works and he also produced operas in several countries. He runs a summer school in Italy and conducts master classes all over the world. Tito Gobbi has recently published his autobiography, *My Life*. 'Cooking is an art,' he says. 'You just have to change an ingredient in a tiny way and it changes everything.'

Appetizer with Green Salad

200 gm fresh tuna fish, chopped finely
1 whole egg
4 tablespoons grated bread
1 tablespoon grated Parmesan cheese
black pepper

Put all the ingredients together and mix thoroughly till well blended. Giving the shape of a thick sausage roll it up in a wet napkin; tie both ends and maybe the middle with kitchen string.

Cook in boiling water on a low gas for one hour. Take it out and let it cool before opening the napkin.

Slice and serve cool with a green salad covered with mayonnaise or a sauce of lemon juice, parsley, chopped capers, olive oil and a pinch of salt.

NB Fresh tuna is difficult to get. This recipe works well with smoked cod or haddock.

Gwynne Howell

Born in Wales, this bass with a notable and mellow voice sings with the major opera companies at home and abroad. He is well known for his roles of Colline, the Monk in *Don Carlos*, the Grand Inquisitor, Philip II, Sparafucile, Sarastro, and King Marke, and for his frequent concert appearances and numerous recordings.

Quick Cheese Grill Plus

FOR 1 PERSON

nice thick Cheddar cheese slices
butter
sliced onion rings
large raisins

Cut Cheddar cheese into good thick slices and cover with blobs of butter. Grill slowly. As cheese begins to crisp and brown, add onion rings or slices to cover cheese almost completely. Add a little more butter where necessary. Add large raisins when almost ready and allow them to swell up in the heat. Then remove from the grill. Eat with side salad of firm tomatoes and lettuce and glass of chilled white wine.

Elizabeth Robson

A Scottish-born soprano who has often appeared with all the British opera companies including The Royal Opera of which she was for many years a member, English National Opera and Scottish Opera in addition to many other companies abroad. Her roles have included Sophie, Susanna, Pamina, Nanetta, Micaëla and Gilda.

Quick Chicken Liver Pâté

8 oz chicken liver
4 oz butter or margarine
herbs: tarragon, thyme, sage, rosemary
4 cloves garlic, crushed
liqueur to suit: 2 tablespoons apple juice, red or white wine,
    vermouth, sherry, port or brandy
seasonings

Remove strings and any discoloration (which makes the pâté taste bitter) from the livers. Gently simmer in butter or margarine. Do not chop the livers as the sides get hard in cooking if chopped. Add herbs and garlic. Cook 5 minutes on either side and turn with two wooden spoons to prevent breaking. Add chosen liqueur and seasoning. Put into a liquidizer until you have a smooth consistency. Place the pâté in a dish and seal with some melted butter.

Soups

Donald McIntyre

Donald McIntyre is a native of New Zealand who has made his home in England. A member of The Royal Opera for many years, he is now known internationally for his Wagnerian portrayals, such as Wotan, Amfortas, Telramund and Kurwenal. He has sung in most major opera houses and appears regularly at the Bayreuth Festival.

From his wife: 'Don is very fond of fresh salads and vegetables. He hates black pudding, and prefers to go without meat, though he enjoys free-range chicken and eggs. He prefers brown to white bread, honey to sugar and is keen on health food shops.'

White Vegetable Soup

FOR 6–8 PEOPLE

1 lb potatoes
½ lb onions
1 lb leeks
2 or 3 Jerusalem artichokes
1 oz butter
1 pint chicken stock
salt and pepper
½ pint milk
2 tablespoons cream mixed with 1 or 2 egg yolks

Peel and clean vegetables, chop roughly and simmer in butter for 5 minutes. Add stock, cook slowly for about 20 minutes. Liquidize, add seasonings, milk, cream and egg yolk. Be careful not to boil after adding egg yolk and cream. Serve with fried croûtons and garnish with fresh parsley or chives.

This recipe freezes very well *before* adding milk, cream and egg.

Roderick Kennedy

Born in England, he has sung predominantly with British opera companies including English National Opera and Welsh National Opera. Currently a member of The Royal Opera, with which he has sung in *Macbeth*, *Otello*, *Ariadne*, *Billy Budd* and *Lucrezia Borgia*.

Asparagus Soup

FOR 4–6 PEOPLE

3 oz butter
6 oz button mushrooms, chopped
1 medium onion, sliced
juice of $\frac{1}{2}$ lemon
bay leaf
3 oz flour
1$\frac{1}{4}$ pints milk
15 oz tin asparagus tips, drained and roughly chopped
1 glass dry white wine
salt and pepper
chopped parsley

Melt butter and cook mushrooms and onions till golden. Add lemon juice and bay leaf, stir in flour and cook for 2–3 minutes. Add milk, asparagus and wine, stirring continuously. Bring to boil. Season and simmer for 10 minutes. Sprinkle with parsley.

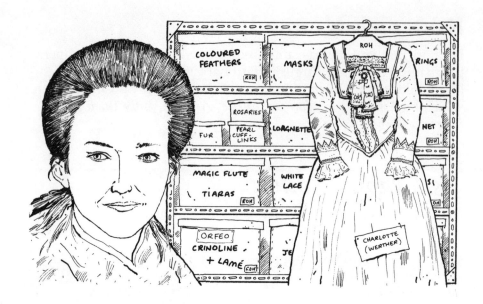

Frederica von Stade

An American mezzo-soprano of wonderful looks and stage presence. Her fine musicianship has been observed in most major opera houses and festivals. She is known for her brilliant sense of comedy particularly as Cherubino, Rosina, Mélisande, Charlotte and Octavian. She has a large concert repertoire and gives many recitals.

Green Pea Soup

FOR 2 PEOPLE

2 tablespoons grated onions
½ oz butter
1 packet (4 oz) frozen peas
1 cup (6 fl oz) consommé
1 pinch thyme
1 teaspoon sugar
1 pinch garlic salt
white pepper
1 cup (6 fl oz) double cream

Cook onions in butter until transparent over low heat (about 5 minutes). Add peas and consommé and simmer for about 10–15 minutes. Add seasoning (thyme, sugar, salt, pepper) and put in blender with cream. To make thinner if desired, add milk. Serve hot or cold, garnished with chives if cold or croûtons or fresh coconut lightly browned if hot.

Isobel Buchanan

Stilton and Onion Soup

FOR 4–6 PEOPLE

1 large Spanish onion
6 oz Stilton cheese
2 oz butter
2 oz flour
2 pints chicken stock
1 bay leaf
salt and pepper
¼ pint single cream

Chop the onion and crumble the Stilton. Melt butter in a pan and add onion. Fry gently until transparent then add Stilton. Stir with a wooden spoon until cheese melts. Add flour and cook for 5 minutes, stirring all the time before adding chicken stock, bay leaf and seasoning. Bring to the boil and simmer for 20 minutes. Remove bay leaf, add cream and serve.

Evgeny Nesterenko

A leading bass of the Bolshoi Theatre, Moscow and known internationally for his deep, rich voice and dramatic acting ability. He has appeared at the Metropolitan Opera, New York, La Scala, Milan, and The Royal Opera, London. He holds the title of Honoured Artist of the USSR. His concert recitals and choral singing are excellent. His operatic roles include many Russian parts – Prince Igor, Varlaam, Boris Godunov and Kochubey – as well as Don Basilio, Raimondo and Philip II.

Borscht

FOR 6–8 PEOPLE

1 lb uncooked beetroots
2 beef stock cubes dissolved in 1 pint water, or 1½ pints meat broth
1 rounded tablespoon tomato purée
2 tablespoons vinegar
1 oz butter
1 onion, chopped
2 sticks celery, chopped
1 bay leaf
12 oz peeled potatoes, diced
12 oz white cabbage, shredded
1 oz piece pork fat
1 clove garlic, crushed
salt and pepper

GARNISH

diced tomatoes
sour cream

Peel the beetroots and cut into straw-like chips. Place in a saucepan with the stock, purée and vinegar. Bring to the boil, cover and simmer for 30 minutes. Meanwhile melt the butter and fry the onion and celery until soft. Add to the beetroot. Cook a further 5 minutes. Add the bay leaf, potatoes and another ½ pint of water. After 10 minutes add the cabbage and pork fat rubbed with garlic and chopped. Stir in another ½ pint water. Cover and cook for 20 minutes. Season with salt and pepper. Serve garnished with chopped tomatoes and sour cream.

NB If the soup is too thick, stir in some more stock.

Richard Cassilly

An American tenor whose career began in New York with Menotti's *Saint of Bleecker Street*. He has worked extensively with the New York City Opera, the Metropolitan Opera, Covent Garden and the Hamburg State Opera. His roles of Laca (*Jenůfa*), Otello, Florestan, Siegmund and Peter Grimes have brought him recognition throughout the opera world. He is a Kammersänger of the Hamburg State Opera, of which he was a member for many years before returning to live in New York.

Yogurt Soup

FOR 4–6 PEOPLE

From 1 pound of ground beef which has been seasoned with garlic, mint leaves, salt, pepper, and some pine nuts (optional) form small bite-sized meatballs. Place these aside. The meatballs may be made up and kept on hand in the freezer, making this soup almost 'instant'.

Using bouillon cubes make a quart of broth. To the boiling broth add a couple of tablespoons of Miskos (Greek hard-grained pasta) and your meatballs. When pasta and meatballs are done, remove from the heat. When the soup has gone off the boil stir in 1 pint of yogurt. Cream yogurt makes a much richer creamier soup but skimmed-milk yogurt is also good. Keep the soup warm, but do not allow to boil or it will separate. Melt ¼ lb butter and add 2 tablespoons of lemon juice and 1 teaspoon of mint leaves. Serve soup with this lemon-butter mixture floated on each serving.

José Carreras

A Spanish tenor of beautiful voice and excellent musicianship, certainly the brightest of the younger generation. His appearances in the roles of Alfredo, Rodolfo, Gennaro, Cavaradossi, Andrea Chénier, Don Carlos and Radamès are amongst those much appreciated by opera lovers. His many recordings include numerous Italian operas.

Sopa de Pescado (Fish Soup)

FOR 4 PEOPLE

1 lb fish
seasoned flour
oil for frying
4 pints water
2 tomatoes, skinned and sliced
1 large onion, chopped
1 red pepper, deseeded and
  chopped

4 cloves garlic, finely chopped
1 tablespoon chopped parsley
2 teacups fine breadcrumbs
1 dozen chopped almonds,
  browned
1 dozen chopped hazelnuts,
  browned

The fish used can be a mixture of bream, whiting, hake, etc., or it can just be one variety of fish. Skin the fish and remove the head and tail. Chop the fish into pieces, roll in seasoned flour and fry in oil. Drain the fish. In the same oil fry the sliced tomatoes, onions, red pepper (stalk and seeds removed) and finely chopped garlic and parsley. Drain the vegetables and add with the fish to boiling water together with 2 teacups of fine breadcrumbs and about a dozen each of finely chopped almonds and hazelnuts which have previously been browned in the oven. The soup is then allowed to simmer and when reduced by about a third is ready to serve. A refinement is to take out the large pieces of fish and to pass everything else through a fine sieve, then replace the fish in the soup, reheat and add salt and pepper as desired.

Rüdiger Wohlers

Born in Germany, this tenor specializes in Mozartian roles, including Don Ottavio, Belmonte, Fernando and Don Ramiro. In addition to his appearances at Covent Garden, he has been heard in most German and Austrian opera houses and festivals.

Bitter Sour Soup (Suan-la-t'ang)

FOR 6–8 PEOPLE

375 gm loin of pork
150 gm bamboo shoots (tinned)
150 gm mushrooms (tinned)
2 onions
3 tablespoons Soya sauce
1 teaspoon flour
salt
pepper
2 tablespoons oil
1 litre chicken stock
2–3 tablespoons vinegar
1 tablespoon starch powder (cornflour)
3 eggs
1 tablespoon chopped parsley

Cut the pork, bamboo shoots, mushrooms and onions into thin strips and place on separate plates. Mix the Soya sauce, flour, salt and pepper and sprinkle over the meat. Warm the oil, and fry the meat in it for 2 minutes. Put the meat into a casserole. Pour in the chicken stock. Add the bamboo shoots, mushrooms and onions. Flavour the soup very sharply with vinegar, salt and pepper. Allow to boil. Thicken with starch powder. Mix the lightly beaten-up eggs into the creamy soup while constantly stirring, not too quickly, with a whisk. If necessary, season again. Sprinkle over the parsley. (40 minutes.)
   This soup is substantial enough to have as a main course.

Robert Tear

Robert Tear is a Welsh tenor who was trained in England. He is
a gifted actor and intelligent singer who has appeared with most
British opera companies and abroad. His roles of Alfredo, Prince
Orlofsky, Tom Rakewell and Peter Grimes are well known and
he created the role of Dov in Tippett's *The Knot Garden*. He has
a large concert repertoire and sings frequently in Great Britain,
North America and Europe.

Chupa

FOR 8 PEOPLE

2 large onions
2 leeks (or bunch of spring onions)
2 green peppers
2 tablespoons oil
4 potatoes
1½ quarts chicken stock
1 lb prawns (preferably raw, but frozen are all right)
about 1 lb white fish if this dish is going to be a main course
½ pint cream
½ lb diced Philadelphia cream cheese

Soften onions, leeks, peppers in oil, then add diced potatoes and
1½ quarts of chicken stock (2 stock cubes). Cook until potatoes
are soft then add prawns (and fish if used). Cook for 10 minutes.
At the last minute add cream and Philadelphia cream cheese,
making sure this doesn't cool the soup.

José Carreras

Gazpacho Andaluz

FOR 4–6 PEOPLE

4 tomatoes
1 small cucumber (8 oz)
1 sweet red pepper
1 onion
3 cloves garlic
salt and pepper
1 teacup (2 oz) fine dry breadcrumbs
3 tablespoons oil
½ teacup (2 fl oz) wine vinegar
½ lb ice

Mince the tomatoes, cucumber, red pepper and onion. Pound
the garlic in a mortar and add the salt, pepper and breadcrumbs.
Then add the oil drop by drop until a thick paste is formed.
Slowly stir in the vinegar and transfer the mixture to the soup
tureen. Add the vegetables and breadcrumbs and stir together. If
a thinner soup is required a little water can be added. It can all be
mixed in an electric mixer and comes out like a purée, or if
preferred, only the garlic, breadcrumbs, salt, pepper, oil and
vinegar and a little water are placed in the mixer and then the
chopped or minced vegetables are added. For any method the ice
is added and the soup left in a cold place before serving. Finely
chopped parsley can be added if desired.

David Rendall

A gifted young tenor, born in London, who has sung with most British opera companies and in major European and North American centres. He has made many operatic appearances at home and abroad in such operas as *La Bohème*, *Così fan tutte*, *Don Pasquale*, *Die Zauberflöte* and *Der Rosenkavalier*.

Cold Basil and Chive Soup

FOR 4–6 PEOPLE

1 oz chives
1 oz basil, fresh or dried
2 oz bacon
1½ oz butter
flour
4 tablespoons white wine
1 pint chicken stock

juice of ½ lemon
6 oz potatoes
salt and pepper
½ pint milk
1 heaped teaspoon Parmesan
4 teaspoons cream

Finely chop chives and basil, putting ⅓ of each aside. Add bacon (finely chopped) to butter, brown the pieces and add the chives and basil. Sweat the mixture for 1–2 minutes and add flour. Continue stirring mixture adding wine, stock and juice of ½ lemon.

Bring to the boil and add peeled and finely chopped potatoes and salt and pepper to taste. Cover and simmer until potatoes are soft. Strain, reserving liquor and adding milk to it. Thicken soup liquor with flour. Put potatoes and herbs through a fine sieve or food processor or liquidizer. Add remaining herbs, put aside. Add the Parmesan and put this stiffish purée back in the liquid and stir until all has been absorbed and it has a creamy texture. Chill in fridge. Serve with a teaspoon of cream in each serving and if you wish, a few finely chopped chives.

This soup is excellent accompanied by a muscadet or rosé d'Anjou.

Charles Mackerras

This Australian conductor studied in Czechoslovakia and now makes his home in London. He has appeared with most leading symphony orchestras and in opera houses throughout the world. His extensive repertoire includes many Czech composers, particularly Janáček. He is responsible for the interest in Janáček's operas in Great Britain. Made a CBE in 1974, he was knighted in 1979 after being Music Director of English National Opera for ten years.

Cold Cucumber Soup

FOR 6–8 PEOPLE

1 lb new potatoes
1 cucumber, sliced
1 small onion
2 oz butter
1½ pints chicken stock
½ pint single cream
salt and pepper

Scrape the potatoes. Reserve a few thin slices of cucumber for garnish. Cut potatoes, onion and unpeeled cucumber into chunks and then sauté in butter for a few minutes. Add stock, bring to the boil, then simmer until potatoes are tender for about 15 minutes. Allow to cool slightly, transfer to blender. When well mixed, remove, stir in cream, correct seasoning. Serve cold, garnished with cucumber slices.

Josephine Veasey

This British mezzo-soprano's gifted voice has been heard in
many opera houses of the world. She has premièred many of her
most distinguished roles with The Royal Opera, London.
Among them are Octavian, Carmen, Eboli, Venus, Fricka,
Cassandra and Berlioz's Dido.

Cold Cucumber Soup

FOR 8–10 PEOPLE

2 large cucumbers, peeled
salt
pinch of sugar
2 garlic cloves, peeled and crushed with ½ teaspoon salt
2 pints natural yogurt
2 teaspoons lemon juice
3 tablespoons finely chopped mint
freshly ground black pepper

Grate the cucumbers coarsely, place in a sieve, sprinkle with salt and leave to drain for at least 30 minutes. Transfer to a chilled soup tureen or large serving bowl, add the sugar and stir in the garlic. Gradually pour in the yogurt stirring constantly, then stir in the lemon juice, two thirds of the mint, and pepper to taste. Taste and adjust seasoning, then sprinkle over the remaining mint and grind a little pepper over the soup to finish. Chill in the fridge until serving time.

John Pritchard

This most travelled British conductor is known throughout the operatic and orchestral world. Music director at Glyndebourne for many years, he is now Music Director of the Cologne Opera. He has made many guest appearances with most major orchestras in Europe, America and the Far East. His many appearances at Covent Garden have included the world premières of Britten and Tippett operas.

Cold Cucumber Soup

FOR 4 SMALL PORTIONS

Cook a chopped medium-sized onion in 2 oz butter for a few minutes but do not brown. Add 3 peeled, chopped and deseeded cucumbers, cover pot and simmer them over low heat until very soft. Put through a sieve and return to pan. Add ½ pint good chicken stock and salt and pepper to taste. Add ½ pint double cream, cook for a few more minutes then cool in fridge. When cold put into thermos containers. Have ready some chopped chives to sprinkle over before serving.

This recipe is ideal for a Glyndebourne picnic, together with Stuffed Duck and Cold Gooseberry Pudding (see pages 115 and 189).

Yvonne Kenny

This young lyric soprano was born in Sydney, Australia, and is now a member of The Royal Opera. She has appeared in Australia, the United States and the Far East. Her main operatic roles include Sophie, Pamina, Ilia in *Idomeneo*, Leila in *Les Pêcheurs des Perles* and Mélisande.

Cold Cucumber Soup

FOR 8 PEOPLE

1 large cucumber
1 large clove garlic, crushed
salt and pepper
1 pint sour cream
1 large bottle tomato juice
chopped chives

Peel the cucumber and chop into ¼inch cubes. Place in a bowl with the crushed garlic, salt and pepper and leave to stand for about 2 hours. Then add the sour cream and tomato juice and mix thoroughly. The soup is best if placed in the refrigerator overnight and served the following day. Sprinkle each bowl with chopped chives.

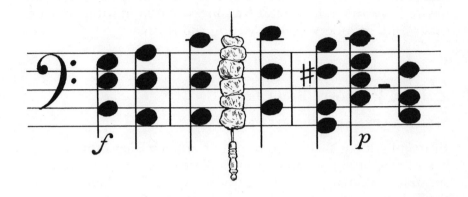

Meat Dishes

Zdzislawa Donat

Born in Warsaw, where she also studied, she has been a soloist with the Warsaw Opera for many years. She is particularly known abroad for her interpretation of Queen of the Night. She has been awarded the title of Kammersängerin in Munich. Her other roles include Violetta, Manon and Rosina.

Zrazy (Rolled Beef Fillets)

ALLOW 3–4 SMALL ROLLS PER PERSON

Beat and salt equal slices of beef. Put on each slice a thin piece of bacon, raw onion, green parsley, a piece of carrot and celery, sprinkle with marjoram, lovage or tarragon. Roll them, fasten the rolls with wooden or metal pins, spread with oil. Put them in a row in an earthenware or glass casserole and roast in the oven at 400 °F for 30–40 minutes.

Serve with buckwheat grits or rice adding to the dish raw vegetables. Bring this meal to the table in the same pan in which it was prepared.

Eva Randová

This Czechoslovakian-born mezzo-soprano, now a member of
the Stuttgart Opera, is known for her dramatic stage presence
and musicianship. Since her arrival in the West she has made her
name in the Wagnerian roles of Fricka, Otrud, Kundry and
others. Her attractive presence, voice and acting ability have
been appreciated in the prominent opera houses and festivals of
North America and Europe.

Filet Žiguli

FOR 6 PEOPLE

600 gm fillet of beef
1 onion
3 tablespoons oil
4 tablespoons ketchup
1 cup cream
salt and pepper

Cut the fillet into strips about 1 cm thick and 5 cm long. Chop
onion and bring it to the boil in the heated oil. Add fillet. Cook
on all sides. Put in ketchup, stir and stir in the cream. Allow 2 or
3 minutes.

My recipe tastes best with rice or noodles. It takes 20 minutes.
Cheers!!

Colin Davis

Music Director of the Royal Opera since 1970 and Principal
Guest Conductor of the Boston and London Symphony
Orchestras, Sir Colin is one of the most distinguished British
conductors. He is particularly well known for his interpretations
of Mozart, Wagner, Stravinsky, Britten, Tippett, Berlioz,
Beethoven and Sibelius. He was knighted in the 1979 New
Year's Honours List.

Boeuf en Croûte

FOR 4–5 PEOPLE

2 lb fillet of beef
butter
2 oz mushrooms
1 dessertspoon chopped
  mixed herbs

½ lb puff pastry
1 egg for glazing
watercress for garnishing

Trim and tie up the fillet of beef, pepper and salt it and brown quickly in hot butter, then roast in the oven for 10 minutes. Slice mushrooms, sauté in butter adding herbs then allow to cool. Roll out pastry and spread mushroom mixture over it placing the beef on top. Wrap the pastry completely round the beef forming a parcel, brush with egg and bake in hot oven (Gas Mark 6) for 20 minutes.

Carlo Bergonzi

A great Italian tenor who is best known for his refined interpretations of Verdi's tenor roles. He has sung most of them in major opera houses and recorded all of them. His international career is particularly strong in the Italian repertoire and his concerts always generate a great deal of excitement. His restaurant, I Due Foscari, in Busseto, near Parma, is named in honour of Verdi's opera and the recipes in this book are some of the dishes enjoyed by its music-loving patrons.

Stracotto di Manzo al Vino Bianco

o rosso (Beef with Red or White Wine)

Take a piece of lean stewing beef, insert slivers of garlic and sprinkle mixed herbs over the meat. Roll in flour, brown in butter, then put in a casserole with wine and beef stock. Simmer for 15 minutes, add tinned peeled tomatoes. Cook slowly over a medium to low heat until done. It will take about 2–3 hours, but the more you cook it, the better taste it has.

James Conlon

A young American-born conductor who has led almost every major orchestra in the United States. His debut in the world of opera, while still a student, was at the Festival of Two Worlds, Spoleto. Since then he has worked often with both American and European companies. Operatic appearances have included the Paris Opera, the Metropolitan Opera, New York, and The Royal Opera, London

Le Tournedos James Conlon

Created for Mr James Conlon by Mr Silvino Trompetto, MBE, Maître Chef des Cuisines, the Savoy Hotel, London.

FOR 4 PEOPLE

4 × 7 oz fillet steaks
2 oz butter
1 teaspoon finely chopped shallots
1 shredded green pepper
½ teaspoon finely chopped tarragon
1 wineglass dry white wine
¼ pint double cream
salt and pepper to taste
1 teaspoon finely chopped chives

Cook the fillet steaks in a thick sauté pan with the butter. When cooked remove to a hot dish for dressing. Meanwhile cook the shallots and green pepper slowly until tender. Now add the tarragon and white wine and cook for a further 3 minutes. Then add the cream, stir with a wooden spoon and cook for a further 1–2 minutes, season to taste. Now pour over the steak, sprinkle the chives over the sauce and serve piping hot.

Patricia Payne

A member of The Royal Opera, Covent Garden, this young
New Zealander with a mezzo-soprano voice has sung in various
roles in major opera houses and festivals, including Filipyevna,
Arvidson, Ulrica, La Cieca, Fricka and Mother Goose.

Roman Beef (With Cloves)

FOR 8–10 PEOPLE

7 oz belly pork or fat bacon
3½–4½ lbs braising beef
6 cloves
25 fl oz red wine
3 tablespoons oil
1 oz butter
1 large onion
salt and pepper

Line the bottom of a deep dish with belly pork or bacon. Tie
beef into a firm shape if necessary and place on top. Add cloves
and red wine. Leave to marinate for 12 hours, turning meat over
once. Heat oil and butter in a casserole. Remove meat from
marinade, wipe dry. Brown on all sides. Peel and quarter onion,
add to casserole, pour in marinade and season. Cover and cook
on a low heat for 2½ hours or cook in the oven at 350 °F (Gas
Mark 4), for the same length of time. To serve, remove string,
carve meat and arrange thick slices on a warm serving dish.
Strain cooking juices and return to the heat. Boil down till
reduced by one half. Serve with meat.

This may seem a spendthrift recipe, but the spoon-tender
meat, perfumed with cloves, is unique and needs only one
simply cooked vegetable to accompany it. Any leftovers are
equally delicious, thinly-sliced, cold.

Nicolai Gedda

Born of Swedish and Russian parents he is acclaimed as one of the great tenors of today. His large repertoire ranges from operetta to the great French, Italian, Russian and German classics, many of which he has recorded. His long career has embraced over seventy roles and he has a masterly grasp of many languages and is a superb recitalist.

Biff Rydberg

FOR 4 PEOPLE

Preparation time about 30 minutes

4–5 fairly big yellow onions	about 2 tablespoons butter
8–10 average raw potatoes	salt
400 gm beef (thick flank or ribs of beef)	white or black pepper
	parsley

When served: 1–2 raw egg yolks per person
according to taste: mustard, HP sauce, tomato ketchup

Slice and chop the onions finely. Peel the raw potatoes and slice them, then cut into cubes. Buy the meat sliced up in about 1/2 cm thick slices, cut it into shreds and then into cubes. Heat the frying pan, melt the butter then lower the heat and fry the onions until golden brown. Remove the onions and keep them warm. Add more butter to the frying pan and fry the meat. When ready it should have a crisp surface. Remove the meat and keep it warm. Fry the potato cubes until golden brown.

To serve, either mix the onions, meat and potatoes or serve separately on a plate. In either case, chop the parsley and put it on top and let 1 or 2 egg yolks slide on without breaking. Season to taste either when cooking or after.

Draught beer goes very well with this dish.

Hildegard Heichele

A soprano of German birth, she has sung primarily in West Germany, Austria, Switzerland and with The Royal Opera. Among her vivacious roles are Adele in *Die Fledermaus*, Susanna and Despina.

Tafelspitze (Gravy Beef)

FOR 4 PEOPLE

Bring to the boil 1 lb soup bones in 3 pints water. When boiled, skim repeatedly. Put in 1 halved onion, unpeeled with 2 cloves stuck in it and 2 bay leaves. Cook on a low heat for 1 hour. Pour through a sieve. Put 1½lb stewing beef into the hot broth; skim when boiled. Add pepper and salt to taste. Cook further in a covered pot on a low heat. After an hour put in 4 chopped carrots, a stick of celery cut in four, 2 parsley roots cut in halves and the white part of 2 sticks of chopped leek. Leave to simmer on a low heat for another 30–40 minutes. The broth can be served with fresh, finely chopped parsley in cups. Serve the beef cut in slices with vegetables, boiled potatoes and green sauce (see recipe on page 154).

Elizabeth Soderström

The Swedish soprano whose fine voice and acting ability rank her as one of the finest singers of today. She is a marvellous linguist, fluent in many languages. She is known for her interpretations of Violetta, Pamina, Tatyana, Leonore, and leading characters in operas by Strauss and Janáček. She is an accomplished recitalist and has recently published her autobiography, *In My Own Key*.

Sailor's Beef

Peel and slice potatoes, put a layer in the bottom of a casserole and some up the sides. Brown slices of rump/sirloin in hot oil with a little salt and pepper to seal the juices. Fill up the dish with alternate layers of meat and potatoes, finishing with potatoes. You can put layers of onion as well and Miss Soderström often uses lager to give extra flavour. Use a stock or bouillon cube to make some liquid. Cover with stock and simmer till the meat is tender.

Serve with lingham berries or beetroots in sour cream or butter.

NB Quantities are a matter of what is required – for example, for 4 people you will need 1½lbs potatoes, 1½lbs meat and 1 lb onions.

Katia Ricciarelli

A gifted young Italian soprano whose singing in both Puccini and Verdi roles is well known. She has sung in opera houses all over Italy, North America, Europe and Great Britain. Her large repertoire includes Lucrezia Borgia, Giulietta, Imogene, Luisa Miller, Lucia di Lammermoor, Amelia and roles in Gluck and Cherubini operas.

Manzo alla Borgogna (Boeuf Bourguignon)

FOR 6 PEOPLE

10 tablespoons olive oil
100 gm butter
salt
pepper
1 kg stewing beef, diced
plain flour
1 kg onions
1 kg potatoes
1 cup broth (stock)
1 bottle dry white wine (burgundy)

Take a deep saucepan and put in the oil, butter, salt, a lot of pepper, and brown. Add the meat, which has been rolled in flour. Brown the meat. In another pan brown sliced onions, diced potatoes, add broth and cook for a few minutes. Add meat to onions and potatoes. Add bottle of wine, turn up heat, cook until done, adding more broth if it dries out. Be careful that potatoes do not become too soft like a purée. When cooled put on serving dish and let it rest for 2 minutes before serving.

Teresa Cahill

An English lyric soprano who made her debut at Glyndebourne before becoming a member of The Royal Opera for several years, in addition to singing with other major British companies and abroad in both concerts and opera. Her repertoire includes Servilia, Pamina, Donna Elvira and Sophie.

Shepherd's Pie

FOR 3–4 PEOPLE

Cut 1¼ lbs best stewing steak (not mince) in small chunks and put in a medium pan. Cover with water. Add salt, ground pepper and a small handful of mixed herbs or *bouquet garni*. Bring to the boil on the stove, then reduce heat and simmer for 40 minutes. In the meantime, peel 3 or 4 medium-sized onions and quarter them. Peel 2 lbs potatoes and boil for 20 minutes in salted water. The meat and potatoes will then be ready around the same time. When the meat is cooked, drain the liquid but save a little of it. This is when I use my Kenwood mincer attachment. (If you haven't got one, the butcher may mince the meat for you and you can chop the onions.) Put the meat through the mincer interspersed with the raw pieces of onion, and let it drop into a large pie dish. Add some Lea & Perrins Worcester sauce and a little gravy made from an Oxo cube crumbled into the reserved meat water. Be careful not to add too much liquid. The meat should be moist, not soggy. Then pour over a large tin of Heinz baked beans. Mash the potatoes with seasoning, butter and a dash of milk and then put them on top. Dot with butter and put into the oven at 350° for 35–40 minutes. Brown under the grill for the last few minutes. It will look as good as it tastes.

A good follow-up is fresh fruit with chantilly cream. Soak strawberries or raspberries in caster sugar, lemon juice and a dash of brandy. Chill in the refrigerator. Whisk ½ pint double cream until it begins to thicken, add ½ oz sugar, some vanilla essence and whisk till stiff. Serve together or separately.

Alberto Remedios

An English heldentenor born in Liverpool, with an outstanding voice. Now a member of The Royal Opera, he was with the English National Opera for many years. Known as Britain's Siegfried, he concentrates on Wagnerian roles, Siegmund, Erik, Walther and Froh.

Chinese 'Mish Mash'

(Quick, tasty and easy)

FOR 4 PEOPLE

1 lb mince
butter or oil for browning
1 small white cabbage
1 small cauliflower
¼ cup cooked rice
1 dessertspoon curry powder
1 small packet frozen beans
2 packets chicken noodles

Brown the mince, slice the cabbage, break the cauliflower into small pieces, then add to the mince with rice and curry powder. Add a little water if needed. Steam for about half an hour or until the vegetables are just soft. Add beans 10 minutes before end of cooking time. Cook noodles separately in salted water. Stir now and then to avoid sticking. Serve with Soya sauce and noodles.

Richard Van Allan

An English bass, Richard Van Allan is a talented actor of gifted voice who has sung with all major British opera companies and is a frequent guest artist in companies abroad. His principal roles include Don Pedro, Baron Ochs, Don Basilio, Würm, Don Alfonso and Leporello.

Babotie (A Malay Dish from South Africa)

FOR 4 PEOPLE

2 slices bread
1 dessertspoon raisins
some milk
1 medium-sized onion
1 tablespoon oil
1 lb lean mince
1 dessertspoon curry powder
1 teaspoon salt
black pepper
1 tablespoon vinegar
1 dessertspoon apricot jam
1 dessertspoon chutney
1 egg
bay leaf

Remove crusts and soak bread and raisins in milk, enough to cover. Slice onion and brown in oil. Add meat and brown. Add curry powder, salt and pepper, vinegar, bread and raisins (with milk squeezed from them). Mix well. Add jam and chutney and mix well. Add a little stock if required. Place in a casserole.

In a cup beat the egg with a little milk and pour over meat. Place a bay leaf in the centre and place in a medium oven for about one hour. The egg mixture will set to form a covering.

Evgeny Nesterenko

'When I am abroad on starring engagements, I am always interested in the national dishes of other countries, but I always pine for the Russian cuisine which I think to be one of the most original and rich in the world. I hold in great esteem those people who know how to cook tastily. A famous singer liked to say before every meal: "One must feed the voice." I presume this saying is not without significance.'

Pelmeni (Dumplings Filled with Meat)

200 gm rump steak
200 gm pork fillet
1 onion
water
salt and pepper
1 egg
225 gm self-raising flour
butter or cream

Mince the meat (best ½ beef and ½ pork) and onion, then add a little water, salt, pepper and mix well.

Prepare the dough separately: take an egg, ¼ of a glass of water (4 fl oz), add salt, mix well with flour and knead it into a stiff dough. The dough should be rolled out thinly. Then with a glass or a metal ring press the dough into small circles. Put on to each circle a small ball of the meat filling prepared as above. The edges of the dough circles should be pinched together into 'half moons'.

Put the pelmeni into boiling salt water and boil them for 10 minutes. Afterwards take them out with a perforated spoon, pour on some hot butter or cream and serve immediately.

Hildegard Behrens

This German soprano, who now lives in Paris, is known for her intelligent interpretations of many roles particularly of Leonore and Salome. A marvellous actress, she has appeared often on film and television. She is also often heard in concerts and recitals, and in the major opera houses of Europe, Australia, and at the Metropolitan Opera, New York.

Pelmeni (Siberian Meat Dumplings)

250 gm minced beef and pork
1 small grated onion
butter or fat
salt, pepper
250 gm flour
1 egg

Cook the mince with the onion in butter or fat. Season with salt and pepper. Knead a dough of flour, egg and a little water. Blend in the meat, flatten the dough and cut into circles with a small glass. Cook well in stock. When served, pepper and a little vinegar may be added.

Elizabeth Soderström

Coaldolmar

FOR 4–6 PEOPLE

Boil a small cabbage in salted water to just soften the leaves. Carefully remove the large outer leaves and plunge them into cold water. Drain and dry. (Use the rest of the cabbage in a salad.) In a basin, mix together 10 oz raw mince, 10 oz cooked rice and plenty of salt and pepper. Wrap small portions of the meat mixture in the cabbage leaves. Arrange in a greased casserole dish, cover with stock and simmer gently for about 40 minutes to cook the filling.

Rüdiger Wohlers

His wife says: 'My husband is fond of food, and he likes surprises for his palate and his eyes. So we often try new dishes, both German and foreign. Sometimes Rüdiger will be at the stove himself, to make up a tasty dish as a surprise for our two sons and myself.'

Königsberg Meat Balls

FOR 4 PEOPLE

250 gm minced pork
250 gm minced beef
   (prime quality)
1 bread roll, soaked in milk
1 onion, grated
½ tablespoon anchovy paste
salt, pepper
½ teaspoon marjoram
2 eggs

FOR THE SAUCE:

40 gm butter or margarine
40 gm flour
½ litre gravy (made from cubes)
2–3 tablespoons capers
1 small glass white wine
juice of half a lemon
salt, pepper
1 teaspoon sugar
2 egg yolks
⅛ litre sour cream

Mix the mince well with the soaked and squeezed out bread roll and the grated onion. Flavour with anchovy paste, salt, pepper and marjoram. Bind with eggs. Make it into 12 meat balls. Bring salted water to the boil, and add the meat balls for about 15 minutes, but do not let them stew or they will fall apart.

For the sauce, warm the butter or margarine, and cook the flour in it. Little by little, while stirring, put the gravy in. Boil up the sauce and leave it to boil for 5 minutes. Add the capers and flavour the sauce with white wine, lemon juice, salt, pepper and sugar. Beat up the egg yolks and cream and mix into the sauce. Warm up, but do not let it boil. Put the meat balls into this sauce.

(About 555 calories per person.)

Agnes Baltsa

This Greek mezzo-soprano is a noted and wonderful musician who has often appeared in the opera houses of North America, Europe and Great Britain. She is famed for her roles of Cherubino, Herodias, Adalgisa, Orfeo, Dido and Dorabella.

Moussaka

FOR 5 PEOPLE

2–3 kg melanzani (aubergine)
salt
oil
1 kg minced meat (beef and veal)
pepper

FOR BÉCHAMEL SAUCE:

2 tablespoons butter
2 tablespoons flour
3½–4 cups milk
salt
pepper
grated Parmesan cheese

Wash the melanzani, cut them across in slices, salt them and cook them in oil till nearly done. Brown the mincemeat in oil with salt and pepper, also till nearly done.

Béchamel sauce:
Warm the butter and make a roux with the flour. Add the milk slowly till it is creamy. Add salt and pepper and the grated cheese to taste. Put the melanzani in a Jenaer glass (Pyrex dish), the mincemeat over it and the béchamel sauce on top. Put some grated cheese and a few pieces of butter over the whole. Cook in the oven at 250 °F for ¾–1 hour till the cream forms a thin crust. Leave to cool slightly before serving accompanied by a light red wine.

Some people prefer to make twice the quantity of sauce and to pre-cook the melanzani in a little oil in the oven instead of on top of the stove. Much success and *bon appetit!*

Riccardo Chailly

This young and promising conductor, son of a composer, was born and studied conducting in Italy. He was Claudio Abbado's assistant at La Scala for two years, and has since appeared in concert and opera houses all over Italy, in addition to the major opera houses of North America, Europe and Great Britain and with the major orchestras including the Berlin Philharmonic, the London Symphony and the Los Angeles Philharmonic.

Créole Meat Pies

MAKES 4 PIES

1 onion
½ oz butter
1 tablespoon olive oil
8 oz choice minced beef
12 oz puff pastry
1 chopped hard-boiled egg
1 oz stuffed green olives, halved
2 oz raisins (soaked in water for ½ hour prior to starting preparations)
salt
pepper
2 egg yolks

Brown the onion which has been cut into small pieces in a mixture of butter and olive oil. Add the meat and cook a little. Take the puff pastry and roll it out until it is approximately 1 cm thick. Form the pastry into a round shape about the size of a smallish plate or saucer. Fill with meat and the pieces of hard-boiled egg, olives, raisins, salt and pepper. Pinch the edges shut. Brush the top with beaten egg yolk, and put in oven, Gas Mark 6, 400 °F, for about 25 minutes or until cooked. These meat pies can also be fried.

Benjamin Luxon

This versatile British baritone is as well known in the opera house as in the concert hall. He has sung with all the major British opera companies and in opera houses abroad, having an extensive range of roles from Ford in *Falstaff*, Onegin, and Tom Rakewell to Falke in *Die Fledermaus*. In concert he is known for his enjoyable renderings of Victorian ballads, in addition to oratorio and Lieder.

Cornish Pasties

MAKES 8 PASTIES

PASTRY

1 lb plain flour
1 teaspoon salt
¼ lb shredded suet
¼ lb margarine
1 egg
water

FILLING

2 lbs peeled potatoes, thinly sliced
1 lb finely sliced onions
1¼ lbs meat (preferably skirt), finely chopped
margarine
salt and pepper

To make the pastry, sift flour and salt and mix with fats. Add egg and enough water to bind dough. Cut dough into number of pasties desired (approximately 8). Roll each piece into an oblong. Mix vegetables and meat together and place on the pastry with a knob of margarine, and salt and pepper, in that order. Wet the edges of the pastry and bring together with floured fingers, pinching and turning edges with thumb and forefinger. Make a slit on the side. Place on floured baking tray in a hot oven (450 °F) for half an hour, then turn down oven (to 300 °F) for a further half hour. Serve hot or cold.

Geraint Evans

This distinguished Welsh-born baritone is famous for his interpretations of roles such as Figaro, Papageno, Leporello, Dulcamara, Balstrode and Falstaff. Knighted in 1969, he has directed productions of *Peter Grimes*, *Billy Budd*, *Falstaff* and *Le nozze de Figaro*. He has always been closely associated with Covent Garden and has had several operas written for him.

Honeyed Lamb

FOR 6–8 PEOPLE

3–4 lb lamb joint (leg or shoulder)
salt and pepper
1 teaspoon ginger
2 tablespoons rosemary
8 oz honey
½ pint cider

Line an ovenproof dish with foil. Wash and rub the joint with salt, pepper and ginger. Place in the dish and sprinkle half the rosemary over it. Cover the top of the meat with honey and pour the cider around it. Cook in a hot oven allowing 20–25 minutes per lb and 20 minutes over. Begin at 425–450 °F, Gas Mark 7 or 8, and reduce to 375 °F, or Gas Mark 5, after 30 minutes. Baste during cooking and add more cider if necessary.

David Rendall

Roast Lamb with Rosemary

FOR 4–6 PEOPLE

1 shoulder of lamb
4 or 5 sprigs fresh rosemary
olive oil
1 tablespoon flour
1 tablespoon cinnamon powder
salt and pepper

Insert a sharp knife into the flesh of the joint and push in sprigs of rosemary (each about $\frac{1}{2}$–$\frac{3}{4}$ inches long). Do this all over the joint at intervals. Rub oil into the meat. Mix flour and cinnamon together with salt and pepper and rub mixture all over the joint. Cook in a hot oven (450 °F, Gas Mark 8) for 15 minutes, then at 350 °F, Gas Mark 4, until meat is medium rare. If you prefer lamb well done then cook a little longer. Serve with ratatouille (page 148).

A good wine to accompany this meal is rosé d'Anjou or if you prefer red with lamb, choose a St Emilion or St Estephe.

NB If you like your meat medium rare, cook for 20–25 minutes per lb (meat thermometer reading 147–150 °F). For well done meat cook for 30–35 minutes per lb (meat thermometer at 160–165 °F).

Josephine Veasey

Braised Lamb Chops in Mint Jelly

FOR 4 PEOPLE

8 loin chops, boned and rolled
1 large onion, peeled and sliced
few mint leaves
salt and freshly ground black pepper
½ pint stock or water

JELLY

½ pint stock from the chops
¼ pint wine vinegar
good bunch of fresh mint leaves, washed and chopped
5 teaspoons gelatine
4 tablespoons very hot water
mint sprigs to garnish

Cooking time: 50 minutes
Oven: 160 °C, 325 °F, Gas Mark 3

Fry the chops in a casserole to brown on each side, without fat. Add the onion, the mint leaves, seasoning and stock. Bring to the boil, cover and cook in the oven for 40 minutes. Remove the chops, cool and place on a serving dish in the fridge. Cool the stock from the chops and skim away the fat. Add wine vinegar and mint. Dissolve the gelatine thoroughly by sprinkling in hot water, add to the mint liquid, cool and pour carefully and repeatedly over rolled chops. Allow to set, garnish with mint leaves. Serve with salad and new potatoes.

Diana Montague

An English mezzo-soprano whose performances have been heard primarily in the United Kingdom at Glyndebourne, The Royal Opera, Covent Garden, and in concert. Her repertoire includes Dorabella, Zerlina and Tebaldo.

Gigot à la Moutarde

FOR 4–6 PEOPLE

English shoulder of lamb
garlic
¼ pint Dijon mustard
2 tablespoons good Soya sauce (not the stuff you get from the local Chinese take-away)
2 teaspoons ground rosemary
¼ teaspoon powdered ginger
¼ tablespoon olive oil

Trim most of the fat off the lamb and loosen the blade bone. Make lots of little holes in the skin and stick shreds of garlic into them, so that the garlic lays under the skin.

For the sauce: blend in mustard, Soya sauce, crushed garlic to taste, rosemary and ginger. When blended together beat in the olive oil drop by drop as if you were making mayonnaise.

Paint the lamb with the sauce, then place on a rack in a roasting tin. Cook for 1½–2 hours at 350 °F or Gas Mark 4. (Cook for longer if you like your joint well done.)

We usually paint our meat a good 2–3 hours before cooking as we like to taste the mustard. Tastes good with anything, but *Gratin Dauphinoise* is particularly good.

José Carreras

Calderete de Cordero (Lamb Stew)

This is a delicious stew from Jerez made with lamb less than a
year old, allowing half a lamb per person.*

For each 2¼lb lamb you need:

wine vinegar
4 tablespoons oil
4 cloves garlic
2 large sliced onions
1 dessertspoon flour
1 glass boiling water
4 peppercorns
1 dessertspoon finely chopped mint
salt and pepper

The lamb is jointed and allowed to marinate for one hour in
equal parts of water and wine vinegar. It is then drained, washed
in clean running water and dried well.

The oil is heated in a large saucepan, the cloves of garlic are
browned in it, then removed and kept. The meat is then added
and carefully browned in the oil, then the sliced onions are
added, together with the flour which is well stirred until the oil
is absorbed. This must simmer over a low heat, when the
boiling water is added, the pan is covered and the lamb is slowly
cooked. Meanwhile the fried garlic is pounded in a mortar with
the peppercorns, the mint and a little salt. A little of the sauce
from the meat is mixed with this and then all is added to the
pan. The meat is removed and the sauce reduced. It is then
poured over the meat, and served.

* This may be difficult to obtain so alternatively use a 2 lb leg of lamb in which case
the recipe would serve 2–3.

Kate Gielgud

Although born in Austria, her training and career took place in England. In addition to her work in the dramatic theatre and television, she has appeared in lyric works such as *Die Fledermaus*, in which she portrayed Ida.

Middle Eastern Lamb

FOR 4 PEOPLE

1 lb stewing lamb trimmed of fat
2 cloves garlic
1 medium onion
1 tablespoon olive oil
½ pint stock made with chicken stock cube
3 teaspoons ground cumin
2 teaspoons cayenne pepper
2–3 tablespoons tomato purée
6 oz chick peas, soaked overnight
2 fresh peeled tomatoes
salt and pepper

Chop garlic and onion finely and fry gently in olive oil for one minute. Add cubed lamb and brown on all sides. Pour on stock and stir. Then add cumin, cayenne pepper, tomato purée, stir and add chick peas and fresh tomatoes. Cook on top of stove for 5 minutes adding more liquid if necessary. Check seasoning. Transfer to a preheated oven, Gas Mark 4, for $1\frac{1}{2}$–$1\frac{3}{4}$ hours.

This dish can be cooked on top of the stove. It is quite hot and can be served with boiled white rice garnished with a sliced banana.

Gwynne Howell

Veal Chops or Pork Fillets Bonne Femme

FOR 4 PEOPLE

6 oz pickled belly of pork or 4 oz rasher of gammon
16 button onions, peeled
4 oz button mushrooms, halved or quartered
4 veal chops or pork fillets
1½ oz butter
1 tablespoon flour
1 wineglass white wine, optional
½ pint stock; use ¾ pint if not using wine
salt and pepper
bouquet garni
3 medium-sized potatoes, quartered lengthwise or 8 whole new
    potatoes
1 tablespoon parsley, chopped

If using pork, put in a pan, cover with water and simmer for 45 minutes. Allow it to cool in the liquid, then drain. Remove skin and cut into ¼inch strips about 1½inches long. Blanch the onions and drain. If using gammon rasher, remove the rind, cut into strips and blanch with onions. Wash and trim the mushrooms, cut if they are too large. Trim the chops or fillets and brown in butter in a shallow pan. Put the mushrooms, onions and pork or bacon into the pan and sauté until golden brown. Then stir in the flour, add the wine and stock and bring to the boil. Season, replace the chops in the pan and add the herbs. Cover and simmer on top of the stove or cook in the oven at 350 °F or Gas Mark 4 for 20 minutes.

Meanwhile quarter the potatoes lengthwise or leave whole if they are new ones. Blanch them and add to pan. Cook for about 20 minutes or until meat and potatoes are tender. Remove *bouquet garni* and dish up chops and potatoes, sprinkled with chopped parsley.

Serve with courgettes *au gratin*.

Francis Egerton

Barbecued Spare Ribs of Pork

FOR 4 PEOPLE

4 spare ribs of pork (English cut)
1 tablespoon oil
1 chopped onion
2 tablespoons tomato purée
6 tablespoons water
1 teaspoon salt

1 tablespoon Worcester sauce
2 tablespoons vinegar
1 tablespoon brown sugar
1 teaspoon dry mustard
pinch of paprika pepper

Fry the chops until golden brown and put into casserole. Mix together in a basin all the other ingredients and pour the sauce over the chops. Cover and bake in the centre of a moderate oven (Reg. 4) for 1¾ hours.

Elizabeth Robson

Galantine de Porc

FOR 6–8 PEOPLE

1½lbs tenderloin of pork (or fillet)
½lb good quality sausage meat
2 spring onions or 1 small onion
zest of lemon (i.e. grated rind)
2 tablespoons fresh breadcrumbs (brown is best)
fresh sage or thyme
seasoning
2 dozen prunes (soaked overnight in wine or cold tea) or 1 small tin
2 cloves garlic
½lb streaky bacon (stretched by scraping lengthwise with knife)

Slit meat down lengthwise the opposite side from skin but don't cut all the way through. Beat out from centre. Lay on half of stuffing (which will be the sausage meat, chopped spring onion, zest of lemon, grated breadcrumbs, chopped herbs and seasoning to taste). Remove stones from prunes and retain the juice. Put a sliver of garlic into the prunes and lay these along the stuffing. Top with the rest of the stuffing and fold over the meat. Wrap the whole around in streaky bacon, place in open foil and cook for 1 hour at Gas Mark 7, electric 425° (a little lower if you have a very hot oven). Leave in turned-off oven for a further 15 minutes to shrink slightly.

For the sauce, use equal amounts of prune juice and red wine (cooking wine is just as good and of course much cheaper). Or if you haven't any wine, cooking stock with a squeeze of lemon. Add 1 clove of garlic and some of the herbs you used in the stuffing. Two prunes will help to thicken the liquid. Boil this until the prunes have rendered down and add some single cream (or the top of two pints of milk), seasoning and perhaps a squeeze of lemon to taste.

The meat slices beautifully and is equally good served cold.

William Elvin

William Elvin made his debut with his native Scottish Opera.
Since then he has appeared with The Royal Opera, Covent
Garden, Glyndebourne Festival Opera and has often made
appearances abroad. His major roles include Leporello, Albert
Herring, Papageno, Figaro, Marcello and Macbeth.

Roast Pork with Oriental Sauce

FOR 6–8 PEOPLE

leg, shoulder or rolled shoulder of pork (about 2½–3 lb)
5 tablespoons Soya sauce (preferably Japanese)
5 tablespoons ketchup
2 tablespoons Worcester sauce
2 tablespoons sugar
2 tablespoons sherry
cornflour

Cook pork in the oven (Gas Mark 6) for ½ hour in a roasting tin.
Pour all the mixture of Soya sauce, ketchup, Worcester sauce,
sugar and sherry on the joint, cover with foil and cook for a
further 1 hour 15 minutes, or until done. Pour the juice from the
roasting tin into a saucepan, skim off the fat, add some
thickening (1 dessertspoon cornflour) and a little water, then
cook for a few minutes. Serve the sauce separately.

John Rawnsley

An English-born baritone who has sung primarily with the
Glyndebourne Festival Opera, Welsh National Opera, at Covent
Garden and English National Opera North in such roles as
Kilian, Ford, Marcello and Masetto. He appears often in concerts
and recitals.

Roast Loin of Pork with Bacon, Prunes and Rosemary

FOR 4−8 PEOPLE

1 loin of pork (about 7 or 8 chops)
½lb dried prunes
salt
¾lb streaky bacon
5 sprigs of fresh rosemary

Soak the prunes overnight and next day parboil them until the
stones can be removed easily.

When buying the loin of pork, ask the butcher to chop
through the bone (but not the meat), so that you can carve the
joint into individual chops. With a sharp knife, remove the fat
and skin from the loin as near to the meat as possible without
cutting the flesh. The rind should then be in one piece. Neatly
score the rind and rub salt into it.

Then cut the bacon into strips, discarding the rind, and lay on
the loin until it is covered. Then cover with a layer of prunes,
followed by the rosemary sprigs and the rind to make a sort of
parcel. The meat should then be put into a pre-heated oven
(350 °F or Gas Mark 5−6) to cook for 25 minutes per lb plus 25
minutes. During the last 15 minutes, the joint should be raised in
the oven and the oven temperature raised to 400−450 °F to get
the required crackling. Remove from the oven and let the meat
rest for 10−15 minutes before carving.

Norma Burrowes

Originally from Northern Ireland, this soprano has sung with every major opera company in the United Kingdom as well as many abroad. Her repertoire includes Sophie, Despina, and Gilda, and she is also well known for her concert and recital appearances.

Pork Boiled in Milk and Garlic

FOR 8–10 PEOPLE

rolled loin of pork (4–5 lbs)
seasoning
garlic to taste (I use 20 cloves)

milk
cream

Season pork. Boil for 4 hours covered by the milk and garlic cloves, skimming occasionally. Reduce liquid by boiling hard until almost dry and add cream for sauce.

Adjust seasoning. Serve with Lebanese Taboulet.

LEBANESE TABOULET

2 tablespoons shallots
8 tablespoons cider vinegar
butter
chives
3 lbs cous–cous
   (corn–meal or burghul)
½ lb chopped green tomatoes
½ lb chopped red tomatoes

1 cucumber, chopped
handful chopped mint
2 handfuls parsley, chopped
handful coriander leaves
salt
olive oil
lemon juice
pimento (chilli pepper)

Cook shallots and vinegar together slowly until well reduced. Add 3 oz demi-salted butter, being careful never to boil the liquid. Add a handful of chives.

Mix everything together and leave for 12 hours.

Gabriel Bacquier

A leading French baritone whose elegant portrayals of such roles as Figaro, Count Almaviva, Don Giovanni, Don Pasquale and Malatesta are well known. His great sense of humour and comedy make him beloved by opera audiences.

Le Cassoulet de Castelnaudary

FOR 8 PEOPLE

For each person: 1 glass white beans
25 grm belly pork rashers
salt
garlic
tomatoes
pepper
bouquet garni
1 piece of confit d'oie/duck (special French tinned goose/duck)
1 piece Toulouse saucisson

On the previous evening, soak 8 glasses of white beans in large bowl of cold water. Cut the pieces of pork into 10 cm × 3 cm strips. Sprinkle with salt, roll them and layer them in a bowl.

On the following day, cook the beans in cold water without any seasoning at all. When they are almost cooked, drain them, rinse them in cold water and leave them in the colander until needed.

Fry until golden two finely chopped cloves of garlic and two pipped and peeled tomatoes. If they are out of season, use 2 tablespoons purée instead.

Place the beans in a casserole, generously cover them with boiling water, add a little salt (the other ingredients will season the beans), plenty of pepper, i.e. ½ coffeespoon freshly ground pepper. Add the tomatoes and the garlic, a *bouquet garni* and finally the goose and pork. Simmer gently on top of the stove for a good 3 hours. It is ready for the oven when the cooking liquid has turned into a light cream.

In a frying pan melt a large spoon of goose fat and gently grill the saucisson for about 5 minutes each side pricking it well with a fork. While this is cooking transfer the beans, goose and pork to a deep earthenware casserole dish. When the sausage is cooked, cut it into small pieces and scatter over the other ingredients. Pour the reserved cooking stock over the ingredients which should cover the beans. Reserve the remaining stock for use later. Put the casserole into a low oven. When a golden crust has formed, pierce it with a fork. See that the liquid has not reduced. If it has, add what is necessary to bring it back to where it was, to cover the beans. Repeat this operation 7 times. For this casserole to be really delectable the crust must be pierced 7 times.

'To succeed with this recipe, it suffices to have a little patience and to *mijoter* with love.'

Zdzislawa Donat

Stuffed Potatoes

FOR 4 PEOPLE

Peel 4 large potatoes of equal size, cut off a thick slice from each, hollow them out with a sharp little spoon and put into salted water to prevent from darkening.

Prepare stuffing made of 8 oz ground veal mixed with 1 fresh egg and 2 oz soaked bread; add salt, 2 cut onions, pepper, pimento or root of lovage (*Levisticum officinale*).

Fill up the hollowed potatoes with this stuffing, put into an earthenware or glass casserole, pour over a prepared broth or meat stock until the potatoes are nearly covered, put a lid on the casserole and stew it in the oven for about 1½ hours. Ten minutes before the dish is ready pour on some sour cream thickened with ½oz flour with added lovage. Return to the oven without a lid and serve hot.

Joseph Rouleau

Joseph Rouleau was born in French Canada where he has been awarded the Order of Canada for his contribution to opera, particularly the Canadian Opera Company. He is known for his special gift in French operatic roles particularly Berlioz's *Les Troyens, Don Quixote, Les Contes d'Hoffmann* and Massenet operas.

La Tourtière

FOR 4 PEOPLE

'La Tourtière is a pie that is traditionally served by French-Canadians at Christmas and New Year. No meals are without this pie at that period. We eat it with all kinds of different condiments: ketchup, little white onions, etc. I believe it is our "creation". It is simple and delicious.'

1 onion, skinned and chopped
knob of lard
¾lb pork shoulder, minced
1 clove garlic, skinned and crushed
¼ pint water
salt and pepper
dash of grated nutmeg or ground mace
little summer savoury, if available
shortcrust pastry made with 9 oz flour and 4 oz fat

Fry the onion in melted lard until soft but not coloured. Add the meat and garlic and continue frying to seal the meat. Add the water and cook uncovered until the meat mixture is almost tender and the texture thick; if necessary, add more water during the cooking to prevent sticking. Add seasonings and flavourings to taste and leave to cool. Make the pastry for the pie plate. Spoon the pork mixture into the pastry case and top with a pastry lid. Seal the edges and make a slit to let the steam escape. Bake in the oven at 240 °C (460 °F) for 8–10 minutes. Reduce heat to 180 °C (350 °F) and bake for a further 40 minutes. Serve hot.

You might think this is a glorified English meat pie, but I believe it is not and I base my judgement on some forty-five years of experience eating this pie at home. *Bon appetit!*

Ileana Cotrubas

A charming Romanian soprano whose vocal and acting talents
are at ease in both tragic and comic roles. She has a large
repertoire, but is especially known for her interpretations as
Pamina, Gilda, Violetta, Mélisande, Norina, Susanna and Mimì.
A fine musician, her recitals and opera perfomances have
endeared her to a world-wide audience.

Sarmale (Filled Vine Leaves)

FOR 4 PEOPLE

1 small onion, chopped
oil to fry
100 gm raw rice
500 gm minced pork or beef
dill, parsley, salt
vine leaves (available in cans, glasses or packets; if they are too salty,
   put in lukewarm water for some hours)
2–3 tomatoes
sour cream

Fry the chopped onion very lightly in a little oil, add rice and
stir; remove from the heat. Mix with meat, add dill weed,
parsley and salt.

Squeeze out the water from the vine leaves and wrap a small
portion of the above mixture in each vine leaf. Lay the sarmale
in a pot, each close together, so that they don't get unwrapped
during cooking. Cover with water, add some peeled tomatoes or
tomato purée and simmer for approximately 2 hours. Serve with
sour cream.

Sarmale are even better the next day when they are warmed
up.

Robert Lloyd

This young English bass is a member of The Royal Opera. He has a glorious voice and is particularly known in Verdi and Wagnerian repertoire. He has also made many guest appearances abroad, and is often heard in concert. He is noted for his interpretations of Sarastro, Doctor Bartolo, the King (*Aida*), Count Walter, Banquo and, most recently, Heinrich in *Lohengrin* and Fiesco in *Simon Boccanegra*.

Nem

FOR 4 PEOPLE

'This is adapted from a Vietnamese dish called *nem*. It depends on the availability of the *nem* itself: it can sometimes be obtained from Oriental grocery stores. Personally we always stock up whenever we visit France. It is worth the trouble because it is one of the most appetizing introductions to a meal that I have ever tasted.'

Nem itself* (a sort of doughy pancake, very thin, almost transparent and crisp when you buy them but when cooked they become soft and sticky).

1 lb ground pork shaped into small balls dipped into egg and flour and fried
1 lemon, thinly sliced and cut into small pieces
4 oz cashew nuts
a few sprigs of mint
root ginger, peeled and chopped
shredded lettuce
1 tablespoon Soya sauce
4 tablespoons vinegar
2 tablespoons brown sugar
½ pint pineapple juice
1 tablespoon cornflour

Arrange the first 7 ingredients in separate dishes. Make a hot sweet and sour sauce: blend together the Soya sauce, vinegar, sugar and pineapple juice and bring to the boil in a saucepan. Mix about 2 tablespoons of this juice with the cornflour and return to pan. Stir continuously over a low heat until the sauce thickens. Simmer gently for a few more minutes.

Cook the *nems* by dipping into boiling water for a few seconds to make them pliable. Wrap up a little pork, lemon, mint, lettuce, ginger, together with a nut or two in one of the *nems* to make a little parcel. Dip the parcel into the sauce and eat using fingers.

Not only is this very delicious, but people enjoy the ceremony of making their own little parcels and they can adjust the contents to their own taste.

---

* An alternative to *nem* is to make small, very thin pancakes.

Lucia Popp

This intelligent singer has often appeared at the Paris Opéra, La Scala, Milan, The Royal Opera, the Metropolitan Opera, New York, and in festivals throughout the world. Her attractive voice, stage presence and acting ability are well known in the roles of Queen of the Night, Sophie, Despina, Gilda and Musetta.

Stuffed Peppers (Plivene Papriky on Slovak)

FOR 4 PEOPLE

4 small green peppers, fresh and blanched
40 gm rice (Uncle Ben's)
200 gm pork, minced
salt
black pepper
green parsley

SAUCE

10 gm flour
1 tablespoon oil
80 gm tomato purée
10 gm sugar
salt
lemon peel
some cinnamon

To prepare the peppers: cook rice, then mix with the raw pork mince and salt and pepper to taste and a little ground green parsley. Stuff the mixture into the peppers and put them to one side whilst preparing sauce.

To prepare the sauce: fry flour in the oil (all in a deep dish which can be used over heat) and then add a dash of cold water and prepare a dark béchamel. Add the tomato purée and more water, sugar, salt and lemon peel as well as a dash of cinnamon to taste and mix together over a very low heat taking care not to burn the sugar. When all is mixed stand the prepared peppers in the sauce, cover and cook over a low heat until ready, for about 1–1½ hours. Serve with plain boiled potatoes.

Donald McIntyre

Piquant Pork Pie

FOR 6–8 PEOPLE

2 lbs lean pork (fillet is nice, but cheaper cuts will do)
2 oz flour
2 oz dripping or butter
½ lb onions
½ pint chicken stock
2 tablespoons vinegar
1 heaped tablespoon brown sugar
salt and pepper
Worcester sauce
1 large cooking apple
12 oz made shortcrust pastry

Dice pork, roll in half the flour and fry gently till meat juices are sealed in. Add sliced onions. Cook slowly for 5 minutes, add rest of flour and then stock, flavourings, and finely sliced apple. Cook slowly till tender. Cover with pastry in a pie dish when cool and cook in a moderate oven, 375 °F, for about 35 minutes.

Gwyneth Jones

The Welsh soprano whose career began at Covent Garden where she sang her first performances of most of her now-famous roles. Acknowledged for her dramatic interpretations of Wagnerian and Strauss roles including Sieglinde, Brünnhilde, Salome, Octavian and the Marschallin, she has sung in the leading opera houses and festivals of Europe and North America and is currently a member of the Vienna State Opera.

Zürcher Geschnetzeltes with Rösti

(Zürich Veal Pieces in Cream Sauce with Rösti Potatoes)

FOR 4 PEOPLE

1 lb tender veal
2 oz butter
2 oz chopped onions
½ lb chopped mushrooms

a little flour
¼ pint white wine
¼ pint cream

Cut the veal into small slices. Melt butter in a frying pan until brown. The pan must be very hot. A little drop of olive oil helps to stop the butter burning and enables you to make the pan really hot. Fry the veal pieces quickly and place on a plate on the side. Now fry the onions and mushrooms lightly, sprinkle flour over them and add the white wine. Stir and let them simmer a little, then add cream. Let the sauce simmer gently until it thickens slightly then put the veal slices back into the pan to re-heat. Do not allow the meat to re-cook. Serve immediately.

Rösti
Boil sufficient potatoes in their skins to serve the number of people eating, preferably the day before. Remove the skins and grate the potatoes into thin strips. Using a non-stick pan, melt some butter and a little oil, put the mass of potatoes into the pan and fry them until a brown crust forms at the bottom. Stir, mixing the browned bits lightly with the top white layer. Smooth the potatoes flat (do not press them together, they should be like a thick pancake), and let them brown lightly underneath again. Place a large round pre-warmed serving plate over the frying pan and turn the Rösti over on to the plate so the brown side is now on top. Serve.

Eva Turner

An English dramatic soprano with immense stage presence and great vocal range. She sang regularly at La Scala, Milan, at Covent Garden, in North and South America and other European opera houses during the twenties and thirties. She was particularly recognized as the great Turandot of her time. Active today, she teaches, judges competitions and is constantly attending performances seeking out new young singers. She was made a Dame Commander of the British Empire in 1962.

Apple and Sausage Pie

FOR 2 PEOPLE

8 oz shortcrust pastry
8 oz sausage meat
1 apple, peeled and cored
1 small onion, finely chopped
1 tablespoon of sweet pickle

Line a small pie plate with half the pastry. Cover evenly with the sausage meat. Chop or grate the apple and onion over the meat and spread the pickle over the top. Cover with the remaining pastry, making a small slit in the top. Bake in a hot oven for 40–45 minutes.

Renato Bruson

Polpettone al Forno

FOR 4 PEOPLE

1 handful soft breadcrumbs (remove crust before crumbing)
milk
50 gm cornflakes
250 gm minced veal
150 gm cooked salami, chopped
1 egg, chopped
3 slices cheese in pieces
1 tablespoon Parmesan
salt and pepper
pinch of nutmeg
seasoned flour
olive oil
4 medium-sized potatoes
2 ripe tomatoes
sliced onion

Mix breadcrumbs in a dish with milk. Crumble cornflakes into mixture. Mix meat with salami, egg, sliced cheese, grated Parmesan, bread and cornflake mixture. Add salt, pepper, nutmeg.

Shape mixture into a long, thick roll, like a very large sausage, roll in seasoned flour and brown in a frying pan in very hot olive oil.

In another pan half boil the potatoes and cut into small squares. Put these in the frying pan with the roll and add chopped tomatoes and slices of onion. Pour over olive oil and cook for half an hour in a medium oven.

93

Luciano Pavarotti

The Italian tenor whose bold dramatic voice is acknowledged as one of the greatest today. He is a magnetic personality known for his wonderful high notes. His performances in *Tosca, La Bohème, Rigoletto, Pagliacci, La gioconda, Luisa Miller* and many other operas are as much sought after as his recital appearances.

Ris de Veau Luciano Pavarotti

FOR 4 PEOPLE

4 whole sweetbreads (blanched and cut in half lengthwise)
flour
3 tablespoons olive oil
2 finely chopped shallots
¼ lb finely chopped white mushrooms
4 peeled tomatoes (cut in four and pips removed)
2 oz San Daniele (Parma) ham (cut in strips)
pinch of fresh thyme
grated zest of 1 lemon, plus juice of ½ lemon
1 wine glass dry white wine

Dust the sweetbreads with flour, and cook them gently with the oil in a thick saucepan until golden brown on both sides, for approximately 15–20 minutes. Now add the chopped shallots and cook for a further minute, then add the mushrooms, tomatoes, ham, thyme, zest of lemon and lemon juice together with the white wine. Cover the saucepan and allow to simmer for a further 10 minutes.

Season to taste and serve piping hot.

This dish was created for Mr Pavarotti by Mr Silvino Trompetto, MBE, Maître Chef des Cuisines, the Savoy Hotel, London.

Richard Cassilly

Kidneys in Scotch

Soak young beef or veal kidneys in salt water, allowing 6 oz kidneys per person. Drain and dry. Remove fat and membranes. Slice about ½ inch thick. Sauté in butter. When almost done add Scotch (to your own taste) and enough fruity sauce to make a thin sauce. Simmer a minute or two and serve with rice.

Ingvar Wixell

A Swedish baritone of strong stage presence who is known particularly for his Verdi and Puccini interpretations, including Scarpia, Rigoletto, and Simon Boccanegra. He has appeared often with The Royal Opera, both in London and on the Far East Tour, and is a frequent guest in European and North American opera houses.

Rognons de Veau Flambés 'Park Lane'

FOR 2 PEOPLE

12 oz veal kidneys or 6 lamb kidneys
1 tablespoon oil
½ oz butter
4 tablespoons brandy
1 medium chopped onion
2 oz mushrooms
1 tablespoon Porto Bianco
salt
pepper
morille powder (½ teaspoon mushroom ketchup)
½ pint demi glace (from a packet if you do not make your own)
chopped parsley
2 tablespoons double cream

When frying pan is hot add a little oil and one piece of butter. Cook the kidneys on both sides for about 3 minutes. Add brandy and flambé. Remove kidneys and put on one side. Add onion and a few seconds later the mushrooms and a little Porto Bianco. When the mushrooms are cooked replace the kidneys, add a little salt and pepper and morille powder (mushroom ketchup). Finally add demi glace and a little cream and mix together. When the sauce is thick, serve sprinkled with some chopped parsley.

Barbara Daniels

An American soprano resident in Germany where she is a member of the Cologne Opera. She has a large repertoire of German and Italian roles which include Susanna, Rosalinde, Violetta, Arabella, Nedda and Pamina.

Liver L'estragon

FOR 4 PEOPLE

4–5 medium onions, thinly sliced
1 clove garlic, minced
3 tablespoons butter or olive oil
1–1½lbs very thinly sliced cubed calves' liver
1 teaspoon fresh crushed estragon leaves if possible (otherwise dried)
1 cup dry red wine
salt and pepper
fresh parsley, chopped

Brown onions and garlic lightly in butter or oil. Add liver (un-scalded) and brown fast and gently on both sides. Add estragon, reduce heat. Add wine, salt and pepper, and simmer for 5 minutes over a low heat uncovered. Garnish with fresh parsley. Serve over white rice.

Daniela Mazzucato

An Italian soprano who was born, studied and made her debut in Venice. She has a very wide Italian repertoire and roles for which she is particularly known include Despina, Rosina and Susanna. She has sung in most Italian opera houses, in North America, Germany and with The Royal Opera.

Fegato Veneziano (Venetian Liver)

Fry 2 onions, sliced very thinly, in $\frac{1}{4}$ cup of olive oil until golden. Add 400 gm good calves' liver cut in thin slices. Fry for approximately 8 minutes. Salt to taste. Serve with slices of toasted Italian bread to dip in sauce. Accompany with vin rosé.

Poultry and Game

Alfredo Kraus

A refined Spanish tenor of Austrian descent. He has appeared in all the major opera houses of the world. His repertoire includes Don Ottavio, Don Giovanni, Duke of Mantua, Werther, Gennaro, Almaviva and Faust. He is highly regarded for his sense of style and his romantic looks lend impact to his strong stage presence.

Pechugas de Pollo a la Espanola

FOR 6 PEOPLE

chicken breast fillets (2 per person)
1 thin slice of Gruyère cheese per chicken fillet
olive oil
butter
sage leaves
beef stock cube
white wine

Beat out chicken breasts thinly and place one thin slice of Gruyère cheese on each.

Roll chicken breast round cheese.

Fry lightly in a mixture of olive oil and butter until golden brown. Add two or three sage leaves, a crumbled stock cube and white wine ($\frac{1}{2}$ glass is sufficient for 6 chicken breasts). Simmer until cooked.

Carlo Bergonzi

Pollo Alla Birra (Chicken with Beer)

FOR 4 PEOPLE

1 quartered chicken
1 tablespoon olive oil
1 oz butter
1 onion
2 carrots
3 pieces celery
1 clove garlic
2 sprigs of sage
2 bay leaves
1 bottle beer
some cream

Brown the chicken in olive oil. In a separate pan, melt the butter and sauté the vegetables and seasonings. Add the chicken, pour in the beer, cover and cook till tender. Just before serving, stir in the cream.

Grace Bumbry

This attractive American mezzo–soprano studied with the great Lotte Lehmann. Her dramatic interpretations and great stage presence in such roles as Tosca, Lady Macbeth, Salome, Princess Eboli, Norma and Sélika (*L'Africaine*) have taken her to the major opera houses and festivals of the world, where she has also given many recitals.

Chicken St Tropez

FOR 6 PEOPLE

4 oz butter
1½ chickens
3½ oz pitted black olives
4 oz green olives
8 oz fresh mushrooms
4 to 6 medium-sized tomatoes
3 onions, sliced thinly
8 cloves fresh garlic
1 palmful basil
1 palmful oregano
1 palmful thyme
2 tablespoons Worcester sauce
pepper and salt to taste
3 heaped teaspoons dry mustard

Melt butter in a pan and add all the other ingredients except chicken. Blend well together. Add chicken, cover pan and cook slowly for about 1½ hours. Uncover for last ½ hour. Serve with rice.

Elizabeth Bainbridge

This British mezzo-soprano has been a member of the Company at Covent Garden for many years, during which she has sung numerous roles and made over 600 appearances both at home and abroad. Her roles include Auntie in *Peter Grimes*, Emilia, Mistress Quickly in *Falstaff* and Filípyevna in *Eugene Onegin*.

Chicken Fricassée

FOR 6 PEOPLE

3½–4 lb chicken, cut into serving pieces
4 cloves garlic, crushed
1 teaspoon paprika
1 teaspoon ground ginger
1 teaspoon salt
½ teaspoon freshly ground pepper
2 oz chicken fat, or lard
2 large onions, coarsely chopped
3 medium tomatoes, peeled and coarsely chopped
1 hot fresh pepper, red if possible
chicken stock if necessary

Rub the chicken pieces with the garlic, paprika, ginger, salt and pepper mixed together. Refrigerate in a covered container overnight. Scrape off the seasonings and reserve. Pat the chicken pieces dry with paper towels. Heat the chicken fat in a heavy frying pan and sauté the chicken pieces until golden on both sides. Transfer to a heavy covered casserole. In the chicken fat remaining in the frying pan, adding a little more if necessary, sauté the onions until golden. Add these to the casserole with the tomatoes, the reserved seasonings, and the hot pepper, left whole and with the stem still on. Cover and simmer gently until the chicken is tender, adding a little chicken stock if there is not sufficient liquid. The sauce should not be watery. Before serving remove the hot pepper.

Richard Cassilly

Jambalaya

FOR 6–8 PEOPLE

Créole is the truly American kitchen resulting from a pinch of Black, French, Spanish and native Indian, blended over a few hundred years. The king of this kitchen is called *Jambalaya*.

1 small boiling fowl
2 pints water
salt and 6 black peppercorns
3 tablespoons olive oil
8 oz cooked ham, diced
4 oz Spanish sausage (cut to bite size)
8 oz shrimps
3 tablespoons (2 oz) butter
1 onion
1 green pepper ⎫
1 celery stalk ⎬ finely chopped
2 cloves garlic, crushed
8 oz uncooked long-grain rice
1 small can (2 tablespoons) tomato purée
1 8 oz can tomatoes
½ teaspoon thyme
½ teaspoon basil
1 crumbled bay leaf
¼ teaspoon cayenne pepper
½ teaspoon Tabasco
salt and pepper
1½ pints chicken stock
¼ pint dry white wine

GARNISH

6 black olives, pitted and sliced
3 tablespoons chopped parsley

104

Place the fowl, water, salt and pepper in a saucepan, bring to the boil and simmer for 30 minutes. Remove the breasts and continue simmering the remainder of the fowl for stock. Chop up breast. Heat the oil and gently sauté all the meats, including the chicken and the shrimps for about 3 minutes.

Meanwhile melt the butter in a large saucepan and fry the onion, pepper, celery and garlic, until onion is transparent. Add the rice and slowly cook until rice browns. Stir in the tomato purée, tomatoes, herbs and spices. Stir in the chicken stock (strained), cover and simmer for about 25 minutes adding more stock if required. Cook until all liquid is absorbed and rice is fluffy. Just before serving stir in the wine and garnish with olives and parsley.

Forbes Robinson

Chicken in Oats

FOR 4 PEOPLE

4 pieces chicken
1 large beaten egg
4 rounded tablespoons rolled oats, seasoned with salt, pepper and
    mixed herbs to taste
4 oz butter

Preheat oven to Gas Mark 5. Remove skin and bones from chicken. Dip into beaten egg and then into seasoned oats. Place in greased casserole dish with knobs of butter. Cover. Cook in middle of oven for 45 minutes approximately. Add more butter if dry. Serve with vegetables and claret.

Zubin Mehta

This noted Indian-born conductor trained in Vienna and is known for his great charisma on the podium. He has been the Music Director of the Montreal Symphony, Los Angeles Philharmonic, Israel Philharmonic and, currently, the New York Philharmonic, having also made guest appearances with most major orchestras. Opera engagements have included the Metropolitan Opera, New York and The Royal Opera, Covent Garden. He has received numerous awards from many countries for his services to music, and his many recordings, in particular India's Order of the Lotus.

Chicken Moghlai

FOR 8 PEOPLE

8 whole chicken breasts, skinned, boned and halved
salt and pepper
flour
½ cup butter

4 medium onions, chopped
4 garlic cloves, minced
1 tablespoon minced ginger
½ teaspoon cumin powder
½ teaspoon turmeric
¼ teaspoon cumin seeds
¼ teaspoon caraway seeds
¼ teaspoon cayenne pepper
1 canned whole green chili, minced
1 lb can whole peeled tomatoes, undrained
2 cups chicken stock or broth
2 pints sour cream
1½ cups brown sugar
1 teaspoon saffron threads
½ teaspoon cardamon powder
¼ teaspoon ground cloves
¼ teaspoon nutmeg
2 tablespoons catsup
2–3 teaspoons dried red pepper flakes

Place chicken on cookie sheet. Season very generously with salt and lightly sprinkle with pepper. Dust thoroughly with flour. Melt ¼ cup butter in a 14 inch skillet. Brown half the breasts until golden on both sides. Remove and set aside. Add onions to skillet and sauté over medium heat until soft. Stir in garlic and ginger and cook for 2 minutes. Add cumin powder, turmeric, cumin seeds, caraway seeds, cayenne pepper and chili. Stir in tomatoes, mashing with wooden spoon. Blend in chicken stock or broth. Return chicken to pan and bring to boil. Reduce heat and simmer uncovered for 8–10 minutes.

Combine remaining ingredients. Slowly stir into chicken mixture. Cook, covered, over a low heat for 30 minutes. Uncover and cook for a further 45 minutes, stirring frequently. Season to taste with salt and more red pepper if desired, and place in a serving bowl.

The sauce will have a curdled appearance, which is proper with this recipe. The texture will be smooth to the taste, however. Excellent cooked in advance and re-heated.

Marita Napier

Marita Napier was born in Johannesburg and is now a member of the Hamburg State Opera. She has sung in most major cities of Europe and the United States. Her roles include Ariadne, Leonore, Elsa, Sieglinde, Kátya Kabanová and Jenůfa, which she has also sung in Czech at the Prague National Opera.

Chicken Piri-Piri

FOR 4 PEOPLE

1 4 lb chicken
salt and pepper
3 large onions
⅓ cup oil
½ cup vinegar
4 tablespoons ketchup
2 tablespoons Worcester sauce
½ teaspoon mustard
½ teaspoon piri-piri (hot pepper sauce)

Boil chicken in enough water to cover with salt, pepper and one large onion. When done, remove chicken, let liquid boil till reduced to almost nothing and add remaining onions, chopped. As soon as these are glazed, add all the other ingredients, let them boil a while and adjust seasoning. Meanwhile, cut the chicken into bite-sized pieces, discarding skin and bone. Heat up in the sauce and serve with rice.

This dish tastes better when prepared ahead and is therefore ideal for large parties.

Roderick Kennedy

Japanese Chicken

FOR 4 PEOPLE

4 tablespoons Soya sauce
6 tablespoons saké (or dry sherry diluted with a little water)
1 tablespoon brown sugar
½oz ginger root, finely chopped
1 large onion
4 slices lemon, finely chopped
1–3 cloves garlic, coarsely chopped
4 large chicken pieces
cornflour
4 tablespoons olive oil

Combine Soya sauce, saké, sugar, ginger root, onion, lemon and garlic. Dust chicken with a little cornflour and marinate in mixture for at least 4 hours, turning occasionally. Sprinkle with olive oil and bake in slow oven (325 °F, Gas Mark 2) for 1–1½ hours basting from time to time. Serve with Chinese rice and a green salad.

William Elvin

Chicken Rice with Sultanas

FOR 4 PEOPLE

1 chopped medium-sized onion
2 tablespoons vegetable oil
8 oz long-grain rice
1 pint of chicken stock (ready seasoned)
small pieces of roast chicken (8 oz–1 lb)
2 tablespoons sultanas
pinch of thyme

In a saucepan sauté chopped onion in oil until tender. Add rice, continuing to sauté until rice grains burst. Add the stock, chicken, sultanas and thyme, put the lid on and continue cooking. When it begins to boil, immediately turn down the heat and simmer until the liquid disappears completely from the surface. Serve hot.

Richard Cassilly

Chicken Tarragon

FOR 6 PEOPLE

Wash, dry, salt, and sauté in butter 6 chicken breasts. Use a pan that may also be placed in the oven. When chicken breasts are brown, remove from flame and pour $\frac{1}{2}$ pint of heavy cream, a good splash of white wine and a pinch or two of tarragon leaves over the chicken. Place in moderate oven for about an hour, basting the chicken with the sauce until all becomes golden brown. Remove from oven, add chopped parsley and serve.

Ileana Cotrubas

Pui cu Ciuperci (Chicken with Mushrooms)

FOR 2 PEOPLE

1 baby chicken
2 tablespoons butter or lard
500 gm (1 lb) mushrooms
1 onion

1 teaspoon flour
stock
salt
sour cream

Cut chicken in pieces and fry in a tablespoon of butter or lard. Separately heat another tablespoon of butter in which you put the washed and sliced mushrooms and a grated onion; do not let them burn. Add the flour and a little stock and leave until the mushrooms are ready. Put the chicken on top, add salt; then cover and put in a preheated oven (375 °F, Gas Mark 5, 190 °C) for half an hour or until the sauce is reduced. Add sour cream to taste. Serve with steamed rice, salad or *mamaliga*, which is the Romanian polenta.

111

Paul Hudson

His opera career has centred primarily in his native Great
Britain, where he has appeared with the major British opera
companies and in such operas as *Der Rosenkavalier, Don
Giovanni, Otello, Salome* and Britten's *A Midsummer Night's
Dream.*

Pheasant Cauchoise

FOR 4 PEOPLE

2 young pheasants
2 oz Normandy butter
1 large Granny Smith's apple, peeled and cored
1 tablespoon plain flour
1 measure Calvados
¾ pint dry cider
¾ pint chicken stock (or stock made from giblets of pheasant)
¼ pint double cream
salt and pepper

Melt butter in a heavy casserole. Add pheasants breast down,
and turn until lightly sealed on all sides. Remove from casserole
and place on one side.

Add the finely chopped apple to the juices remaining in the
casserole. Cook until soft.

Over a very low heat, add the flour and stir until it dissolves.
Return pheasants to the casserole, raise heat and add Calvados.
Ignite the liquid and flambé.

Add cider and stock, stir, cover casserole, and leave to bubble
gently for ¾ hour. Do not allow the sauce to boil.

Before serving, remove pheasants and carve. Add double
cream to the sauce, bring to the boil then strain. Taste and
season. Serve the sauce hot over the carved pheasants.

A lightly chilled Muscadet or still cider should accompany the
above dish.

Josephine Barstow

Mimì, Violetta, the Countess Almaviva, Salome, Lady Macbeth, Jenůfa and many other roles have taken this talented English soprano to distinguished opera houses in England and abroad, where she is known for her sensitive and dramatic interpretations.

This recipe was given to Josephine Barstow by her dresser, with interspersed recommendations by the wig lady, when she asked them for a typical Piedmontese lunch to give to her family who joined her in Turin for Christmas while she was singing Lady Macbeth. Family verdict – delicious!

Guinea Fowl Piedmontese

FOR 4–6 PEOPLE

1 guinea fowl	1 clove garlic
2 pieces celery	1 piece rosemary
1 onion	2 or 3 leaves sage
1 carrot	salt and pepper
3½oz very very thinly sliced streaky bacon	1 glass dry white wine
1 tablespoon oil	watercress
1 oz butter	truffle

Cut up all the vegetables very finely into tiny squares, also one slice of the bacon and the liver of the guinea hen. Put olive oil and a little butter into a saucepan and add all this (it's called *tritato*) and cook slowly for a short time.

Wash and dry the bird, put garlic, rosemary and sage inside it, sprinkle liberally with salt and pepper and wrap it up in the bacon. Place in an ovenproof dish on top of the *tritato*. Put in oven, turning from time to time and basting it with the *tritato*. When it's nicely browned put in a glass of dry white wine, shake it a bit, then cover and cook for an hour in a slow oven. Don't let it dry out. Add hot water if necessary and keep basting with the sauce of *tritato*.

To serve, decorate with watercress and sprinkle with a finely chopped truffle.

113

Carol Neblett

A striking American-born soprano who appears often with the major American opera companies. She also has been heard at the Vienna State Opera and The Royal Opera House, Covent Garden. Her repertoire includes Violetta, Leonore, Countess Almaviva, Desdemona and Minnie in *La fanciulla del West*.

Holiday or Opera Duck (Turandot Style)

FOR 3–4 PEOPLE

To roast a 4–5 lb duck: sprinkle the inside of the duck with Soya sauce, freshly ground white pepper and salt. Add to the inside of the duck 2 large cloves of garlic (thinly sliced), tart apple slices, 3 tablespoons medium sherry and seedless raisins which have been soaked in brandy overnight. I use cognac. Place the duck on a rack in a large casserole and baste it with sherry, honey, Soya sauce and butter.

To crisp the skin I begin with the oven at a very high temperature and then reduce the temperature after 15 minutes to 350 °F for 2 hours, always basting as the duck is roasting. Be sure and poke the duck with a sharp fork every 20 minutes so that the fat runs into the pan and can be skimmed off.

For a sauce I make home-made mayonnaise and add 2 tablespoons Jamaican ground ginger to a quart of mayonnaise with 1 cup of whipping cream and the sauce from the duck gravy (no fat!). Mix these ingredients in a blender. Add salt, honey and lemon to your own taste.

I served this duck to Tony Randall after his tour of *The Odd Couple* and it was a great success! Serve it with a spinach, fresh mushrooms and walnut salad with an oil, vinegar and herb dressing. Serve fresh fruit and cheeses for dessert as the duck is *very* rich and requires little accompaniment.

114

John Pritchard

Stuffed Duck

FOR 4 PEOPLE

Ask your butcher to bone a large duck (or do it yourself). Chop 2 onions very finely and cook slowly for a few minutes. Add $\frac{3}{4}$lb minced veal, $\frac{3}{4}$lb minced pork and $\frac{1}{2}$lb calves' liver, also minced. Cook until all meat has heated through. Add salt and pepper and a generous amount of chopped fresh herbs that might be available (tarragon, parsley, sage, marjoram or thyme). If it is too early in the season for fresh herbs, add $\frac{1}{4}$lb chopped mushrooms. Finally add a small wine glass of brandy. Stuff the duck with this mixture so that it assumes as near as possible the original shape. Tie the ends with string and roast in a medium oven for approximately $1\frac{1}{2}$ hours or until cooked through. Drain duck on a wire rack to get rid of all the surplus fat and allow to cool. When cold it is easy to cut into slices for a picnic and all you need to go with it is a tomato salad liberally scattered with chopped basil.

This recipe is ideal for a Glyndebourne picnic, together with Cold Cucumber Soup and Cold Gooseberry Pudding (see recipes on pages 47 and 189).

Richard Cassilly

Venison

FOR 6–8 PEOPLE

1 3–4 lb venison roast (saddle or haunch)
juice of 3 lemons
juice of 1 orange
garlic
pepper
2 fl oz olive oil
instant potato powder to thicken
salt
vinegar
cranberries } or Cumberland sauce

Place venison in roasting pan and pour over the juice of the lemons and orange with a generous amount of garlic and pepper ... *no salt*. Pour 1 cup of water and ¼ cup of olive oil around roast (or rub roast with olive oil before placing it into the pan). Bake at 350 °F or 177 °C for ½ hour per pound. Baste every ½ hour. Add water when needed. Make sauce with potato powder and drippings. Add salt, a couple of tablespoons of canned cranberries and a small amount of vinegar *or* that quantity of Cumberland sauce.

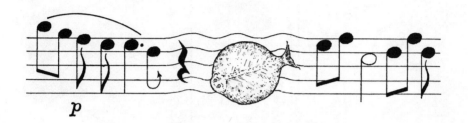

Fish Dishes

Martina Arroyo

This North American soprano is best known for her roles of Aida, Leonore, Elsa, Elvira, and Norma, which she has sung in all the major opera houses of the world. She has also appeared with many major orchestras in concerts and festivals.

Fresh Crab Dish

FOR 2–3 PEOPLE

1 lb fresh lump crab meat, cooked
olive oil
2–3 sections garlic clove, chopped
⅓ cup each chopped onion,
   green pepper, celery
salt and black pepper

2 teaspoons oregano
1 bouillon cube (chicken or beef)
1 teaspoon chopped parsley
Tabasco sauce
grated Parmesan cheese or
   breadcrumbs

Heat enough olive oil to cover bottom of skillet. Sauté slowly garlic, chopped onion, green peppers and celery. Add salt, black pepper to taste and oregano. Add bouillon cube, parsley and touch of Tabasco sauce. At last minute toss in 1 lb of fresh lump crab meat to soak up sauce, then cover with grated Parmesan cheese or breadcrumbs and bake in a medium oven until cheese is melted and brown. Serve piping hot.

Agnes Baltsa

'I cook only for fun and for the pleasure of it, and only when I am in a good mood. It is a pastime. I enjoy reading cookbooks from time to time, but I never cook any of their recipes. I discover my own recipes for amusement.'

Fish Dish (It has no name; it is my invention.)

FOR 3−4 PEOPLE

200 kg crab meat (fresh or deep frozen)
olive oil
salt and pepper
1 can Pilsen
600 kg sole
1 small glass dry sherry
a little flour

Allow the crab to marinate in a pot with the oil, salt, pepper and Pilsen. Add a little water and cook until almost soft. Rub the sole with sherry. Add to the pot and cook until fish is soft. Blend a little flour with water and add it to the pot to thicken the liquor. I serve it with parsley, potatoes and white wine.

Michael Langdon

A much-loved British bass who has sung his vast repertoire in major opera houses throughout the world. A member of The Royal Opera for over twenty years, he is best known as Baron Ochs, Claggart, Méphistophélès, Osmin, Bottom, the Grand Inquisitor, in addition to many other roles. He was recently appointed head of the National Opera Studio, London.

Mussels Marinière (Cooking time 10 minutes)

FOR 3 PEOPLE

2 pints mussels
1 small onion
3 pieces celery
1 bunch parsley
1 tablespoon tarragon vinegar
dry white wine to taste
seasoning
chopped parsley

Scrub mussels thoroughly, discarding open ones. Put into a large saucepan together with water and add onion, celery, parsley, vinegar, white wine, salt and pepper to taste. Heat slowly until mussels open. Drain mussels retaining the liquor. Remove any weed growth and the beards. Remove top half of shell, leaving mussels on the other half shell. Reboil the liquid, strain, and pour over the mussels. Sprinkle chopped parsley over the mussels.

Serve with fresh French bread and butter, together with a bottle of good dry white wine.

Paul Crook

Paul Crook is now a member of The Royal Opera, Covent Garden, after having spent a period with the English National Opera. His character roles include Mime in Wagner's *Ring* Cycle, Monostatos in *Die Zauberflöte*, Don Basilio, Herod and Valzacchi.

Shrimp Créole

FOR 3-4 PEOPLE

1 lb shrimps, peeled
1 large onion
2 large celery stalks
1 tablespoon chopped parsley
1 bell pepper (a small, red, very hot pepper)
2 tablespoons bacon dripping
1 3½oz can tomato paste
¼ pint water
salt and pepper
2 bay leaves
3 cloves garlic
½ tablespoon thyme

Clean the shrimps. Chop onion, celery, parsley and bell pepper. Put bacon dripping in a large skillet and sauté all vegetables until slightly browned. Add tomato paste and water and simmer till thick. Add shrimps, salt, pepper and seasonings and simmer till shrimp is thoroughly hot but still firm. If the mixture is too dry, add some more water. Stir gently from time to time and serve over rice.

Grace Bumbry

Shrimp Créole in Spinach-and-Rice Ring

FOR 6 PEOPLE

1 small onion, sliced
2 parsley sprigs
½ lemon, sliced
2 teaspoons salt
3 whole black peppers
1½ lbs raw shrimps, shelled and deveined
1 1 lb can tomatoes, undrained
1 8 oz can tomato sauce
1 teaspoon Worcester sauce
1 teaspoon salt
1 dash pepper
1 bay leaf

CRÉOLE SAUCE

¼ cup butter or margarine
¼ cup chopped onion
¼ cup coarsely chopped green pepper

SPINACH–AND–RICE RING

4 cups cooked rice
½ cup finely chopped spinach
2 tablespoons butter or margarine, melted

In a large saucepan, combine 1 quart water, the sliced onion, parsley sprigs, lemon, salt and black peppers. Bring to the boil. Add the shrimps, bring back to the boil and simmer, covered, for 5 minutes or until just tender. Drain shrimps; set aside until ready to use.

Meanwhile preheat the oven to 350 °F. Butter a 5-cup ring mould.

Make Créole sauce: in a large skillet, melt butter and sauté onion and green pepper until onion is golden (about 5 minutes). Add tomatoes, tomato sauce, Worcester sauce, salt, pepper, and bay leaf; bring to the boil. Reduce heat and simmer, uncovered, for 10 minutes. Remove and discard bay leaf.

Add shrimps to the sauce; simmer, covered, for 15 minutes, or until shrimps are hot.

Meanwhile, prepare spinach-and-rice ring. In a large bowl, combine rice, spinach and melted butter; toss until well blended. Pack lightly into mould, smoothing the top. Bake for 10 minutes, or till heated.

To serve: run small spatula around edge of mould; invert on to warm serving platter. Fill centre with shrimps and sauce.

José Carreras

Langosta a la Catalana 1

(Crayfish from Barcelona)

FOR 2 PEOPLE

1 medium-sized crayfish cut in pieces
oil for frying
2 tablespoons finely chopped onion
6 tomatoes peeled and seeded
2 sweet red peppers, baked, skinned and cut in strips
½ tumbler white wine
2 dessertspoons chopped parsley
½ teaspoon saffron
1 tablespoon cognac
½ teaspoon cayenne pepper
4 small slices fried bread

The crayfish is cut up and fried quickly in very hot oil, then taken out and drained. The onions are fried in the same oil, then the tomatoes and peppers are added and fried. The crayfish is then returned to the pan with the white wine, parsley and saffron and allowed to simmer for half an hour. The crayfish is removed and the sauce is reduced over a strong heat. The cognac is lighted in a warm soupspoon and put into the sauce with the cayenne. The crayfish is placed on a serving dish, the sauce poured over it and the dish surrounded by slices of fried bread.

Langosta a la Catalana 2

(Crayfish from Lerida)

FOR 2 PEOPLE

1 crayfish of about 2¼ lbs

The crayfish is split in half. It is seasoned with salt, black pepper and lemon juice, smeared with oil and grilled.

SAUCE

12 almonds roasted in the oven
2 cloves garlic
½ teaspoon black pepper
½ teaspoon red pepper
1 teaspoon parsley
2 tomatoes, skinned and seeded
juice of 1 lemon
2 tablespoons vinegar
2 coffeecups olive oil

All the ingredients are ground together in a mortar and served with the crayfish.

Charles Mackerras

Filets de Sole Véronique

FOR 6 PEOPLE

1½lbs filleted Dover soles
1 small onion
seasoning
bouquet garni
¼ pint dry white wine
½lb white grapes
1 oz butter
1 tablespoon flour

Boil the fish trimmings and bones for 20 minutes covered in 1 pint water with chopped onion and seasoning. Uncover, and reduce the stock by half. Put fillets in an oven dish, add *bouquet garni*, and cover with equal parts of fish stock and white wine. Bake for 20 minutes in a medium-low oven (320 °F, Gas Mark 3). Meanwhile, peel, halve and stone the grapes. Melt butter until foaming, stir in flour and add liquid in which the fillets were baked. Boil and adjust for consistency. The sauce should be creamy. Add the grapes, reserving a few for garnish. Pour the sauce over the fillets and serve.

José Carreras

Atun o Bonito con Tomates

(Tuna with Tomatoes, from Huelva)

FOR 4–6 PEOPLE

2¼lbs tuna (or cod)
salt and pepper
oil for frying
1 onion, finely chopped
3 cloves garlic, finely chopped
3 tomatoes, seeded and skinned
1 tumbler white wine
1 tablespoon chopped parsley
½ cup breadcrumbs
1 teaspoon paprika
1 teaspoon sugar

The fish is cut in thick steaks, seasoned and fried in a frying pan with as little oil as possible. In another saucepan the onion and garlic are slowly cooked in oil and then the tomatoes are added, together with the white wine and parsley. The whole mixture is covered and simmered slowly for 2 hours. Then the fish is drained well and put in a casserole or oven dish. The breadcrumbs are then slowly fried in the oil in which the fish was cooked, and when nicely browned the paprika is added. This is then added to the tomato mixture and everything is stirred well. This thick sauce is now passed through a sieve, seasoned with salt and pepper and sugar, then poured over the fish, which is cooked uncovered in the oven for about 10 minutes and then served in the same dish.

Elizabeth Soderström

Grav Lax

FOR 6–8 PEOPLE

Take the thickest part of the salmon (about 1 kg middle-cut piece), and cut the flesh off the bones, so that you have 2 fillets with the skin on. Mix together 100 ml each of salt and sugar and lots of chopped fresh dill. Put one fillet skin-side down in a large flat dish with sides, and pile on top the salt, sugar and dill mixture. Put the other fillet on top like a sandwich. On top put more of the mixture, then weight with a plate to hold it together and leave it for a minimum of 24 hours.

NB This is a traditional Swedish dish. The salt and sugar have the effect of curing the salmon, which is then sliced thinly and eaten without its being cooked and with black bread to mop up the sauce.

Sauce for Grav Lax

Take some Swedish mustard which is slightly sweet. Dilute with oil, vinegar and sugar (if you are a really bad Swede), salt and pepper.

Add some of the finest parts of dill and stir.

Geraint Evans

Trout with Almonds

FOR 2 PEOPLE

2 rainbow trout
4 oz butter
salt and freshly ground pepper
juice of ½ lemon
2 oz flaked almonds
¼ pint single cream
parsley to garnish
whole toasted almonds

Defrost trout and wash, remove fins. Place the butter in a grill pan under a medium heat to melt. Lay the trout in the melted butter, then season with salt, freshly ground pepper and lemon juice. Sprinkle with flaked almonds and place under the grill for 8 minutes turning once. Remove and allow to drain. Add the cream to the melted butter and return to the grill. Allow the mixture to heat through until it thickens. Lay the trout on a serving dish, spoon the cream mixture over and garnish with the parsley and toasted almonds before serving.

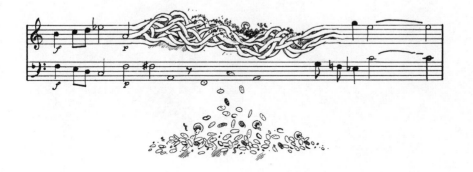

Pasta and Rice

Katia Ricciarelli

Risotto allo Champagne (Champagne Rice)

FOR 6–8 PEOPLE

4 tablespoons olive oil
50 gm butter
1 lb raw rice
¼ litre bottle Champagne
6 coffeecups white wine
approx 2 pints hot broth (stock)
1 cup single cream
Parmesan cheese, grated

Melt oil and butter till golden and add the rice slowly. Stir constantly for several minutes, add Champagne, stir until rice is dry. Then add white wine. Slowly add broth, and when half cooked (7 minutes), add cream and keep stirring. Do not cook over 16 minutes. Rice must be thick, but very soft. Put in a warmed dish and sprinkle with Parmesan.

Peter Maag

Risotto Rusticano

FOR 4 PEOPLE

½ chopped onion
1 sausage cut into pieces
5 tablespoons olive oil
8 handfuls Italian brown rice
½ litre stock made from Knorr or Oxo cube
1 small chilli
3 bunches red radishes
1 teaspoon salt
ground pepper
4 spoons grated Parmesan cheese

Brown the onion and sausage in oil and add the rice. Stir until golden, add chilli then add stock, little by little, until rice is cooked. It takes about 20 minutes and should be moist. Brown radishes in oil and salt and add rice along with ground pepper and Parmesan cheese. Serve hot.

Garcia Navarro

Spanish-born, this conductor has conducted the London Symphony and the London Philharmonic Orchestras, in addition to The Royal Opera in London. He is now Music Director of the National Theatre of San Carlos in Lisbon.

Paella a la Valenciana

FOR 6 PEOPLE

A paellera is a pan especially designed for cooking paella. It should be as fat and smooth as a frying pan.

1200 gm chicken, or half a chicken or half a rabbit
125 cc olive oil
250 gm green beans
200 gm garrofan, a type of flat white haricot bean (if you cannot find them, they can be omitted)
250 gm ripe tomatoes
water, 3 parts water to 1 part rice
a sprig saffron
600 gm rice
juice of 1 lemon
salt

Season the meat with salt, fry in warmed oil. When the meat takes on a golden colour, add the green beans and garrofan and when these are sufficiently fried, add the tomato, always watching the meat so that it does not become burnt. Add the water, turning up the heat, and leave it to cook for 20 minutes. During this cooking salt to taste and add the saffron. When the 20 minutes is up, add the rice distributing it equally over the entire frying pan, leaving it to cook for 10 minutes over a strong heat and 10 minutes over a slow heat, watching continuously. Add more water if necessary, but it is preferable not to. When the rice mixture is cooked remove from the heat, waiting 5–10 minutes before serving. Squeeze the juice of a lemon over the dish before serving, according to taste.

The above is a traditional Paella Valenciana but one can always vary it by using rabbit or seafood instead of chicken. A mixture of chicken and rabbit or chicken and seafood is also to be recommended.

Domenico Trimarchi

This Italian baritone has appeared in most major opera houses in
Europe, North America and Great Britain. His character roles
are many and varied, including Melitone, Doctor Bartolo and
Dulcamara.

Risotto di Pesce

FOR 6 PEOPLE

Put 3 tablespoons sunflower seed oil into a frying pan. Add a
section of a garlic bud cut into small pieces and a pinch of salt.
Fry lightly. Add a small amount of chopped parsley. Cover the
pan and cook until garlic pieces are golden brown, *not* fried. Add
150 gm mushrooms cut into small pieces, 150 gm cooked
shrimps, 150 gm cooked mussels (without shells), 150 gm
cooked clams. Reserve ¾ pint juice that shrimps, clams and
mussels have been cooked in. * Add a small amount of this to the
above mixture, cook for 5 minutes. Add 150 gm dry rice, not
washed. Stir, slowly add juice and cook for 20 minutes, then add
more parsley. When the rice is cooked, the mixture should be
soft. Add 1 tablespoon butter before serving.

* In the absence of such a fish stock, use a lightly flavoured chicken stock.

Fiorenza Cossotto

An Italian mezzo–soprano who has appeared extensively in Italy and in all the major opera houses of the world. Roles she is particularly known for include Eboli, Azucena and Amneris.

Panissa

'A dish I would like you to know is called *Panissa*. It is typical of Piedmonte, where I was born. The ingredients are all locally produced and the dish should be served with a wine from the region like Barolo or Barbera.'

FOR 2 PEOPLE

½ onion, chopped
a little butter
a little olive oil
a little lard
100 gm fresh salami

1 ripe tomato, chopped
½ kg beans, if fresh (200 gm if dry)
6 coffeecups rice
salt
Parmesan

Take a large casserole, fry the onion with butter and oil, then add the fat and salami, then the tomato.

In a separate pan cook the beans in water and keep the liquor. (If using dry beans, soak them the night before.) Remove beans.

Now add the rice to the salami mixture with a little of the bean liquor and stir so it does not stick to the pan. While the rice cooks, keep adding the bean liquor. When the rice is almost cooked add the beans, some butter and a pinch of salt to taste. Transfer to a serving dish and sprinkle with Parmesan.

Kiri te Kanawa

This beautiful soprano, who grew up in her native New Zealand, now makes her home in England. A leading star at Covent Garden, whose visits to other international opera houses are equally prized, her glorious voice has captivated many hearts, singing such roles as Micaëla, Mimì, Countess Almaviva, Fiordiligi, Donna Elvira, Rosalinde, Violetta, Arabella, Tatyana and Amelia (*Simon Boccanegra*). She has also done much concert, television and film work, including the Losey film of *Don Giovanni*.

Bacon & Egg Pie

FOR 4–6 PEOPLE

6 oz flaky pastry
4 rashers bacon
5 or 6 eggs
pepper and salt
1 grated onion

Roll out half the pastry and line an enamel or tin plate with it. Cover with bacon, cut into neat pieces. Break in the eggs keeping them whole. Sprinkle with pepper and salt and grated onion. Roll out other half of pastry and cover. Bake for about 15 minutes at Gas Mark 6, 400 °F and for 30 minutes at Gas Mark 4, 350 °F.

Peter Maag

Spaghetti del Marinaio (Seaman's Spaghetti)

FOR 4–6 PEOPLE

1 small green chilli
1 clove garlic
6 tablespoons olive oil (1 for the water that you boil the spaghetti in)
2 7½oz cans peeled tomatoes, sieved
1 can tuna fish
6 fillets of anchovy
½ cup salted capers
1 cup black olives
3 teaspoons oregano
dash of ground pepper
3 teaspoons chopped parsley
2 teaspoons salt
500 gm spaghetti

Brown the chilli and garlic in 5 tablespoons oil. When the garlic is golden add the peeled tomatoes which have been passed through a sieve. Stir for a few minutes, then add tuna fish, anchovies, capers, olives, oregano and ground pepper. Let the sauce thicken then add parsley at last minute.

Boil water, add salt, 1 tablespoon oil then spaghetti. When *al dente* (spaghetti should be slightly underdone, a bit hard), strain and mix in a bowl with sauce. Serve very hot.

Domenico Trimarchi

Linguine con Capri e Olivi Neri

(Linguine with Capers and Black Olives)

FOR 2 PEOPLE

Into a frying pan put 4 tablespoons sunflower oil, add a section of a garlic bud cut into small pieces and 150 gm tomatoes. When these are cooked add 50 gm capers and 100 gm black olives without the pips. In another utensil add to boiling water 150–200 gm of linguine or linguinetti. * Cook *al dente*. Add sauce, stir and put into a warm bowl.

* If linguine is difficult to obtain, use spaghetti instead. This will be thinner but just as good.

Anne Pashley

Savoury Pasta

FOR 2–4 PEOPLE

2 onions
2 oz butter
½ lb mushrooms
handful of chopped parsley
½ cup breadcrumbs
½ large tin Italian tomatoes (15½ oz)
1 dessertspoon tomato purée
large garlic cheese e.g. Boursin
½–¾ lb noodles
Parmesan cheese

Sauté onions in butter and after a few minutes add the mushrooms and parsley. Stir until they are beginning to cook then reduce heat, cover and simmer for about 10 minutes. Add breadcrumbs and mix in with the tomatoes and tomato purée. Simmer for another minute or two and then turn off the heat and add the garlic cheese in pieces. Melt this slowly. Cook the noodles till ready and put in ovenproof dish. Turn in the mixture and scatter with grated Parmesan cheese. Bake in the oven at Gas Mark 4 for 10 minutes or so and serve. We use fungi collected in beechwoods for the recipe but you need to be careful which you pick!

Donald Gramm

An American bass-baritone who has appeared in many of the world's opera houses, festivals and the concert stage. He is well known for his character interpretations, particularly of Don Alfonso, Leporello, Don Pasquale and Nick Shadow.

After-the-Opera Supper Dish

FOR 20–24 PEOPLE

3½lbs minced beef
3 medium-sized onions
1 large green pepper
2 large cans tomatoes
1½ teaspoons dried oregano
1½ teaspoons dried basil
2 teaspoons salt
½ teaspoon pepper
2 lbs Cheddar cheese
1 jar prepared marinara sauce
2 packages small pasta shells

Sauté minced beef in a skillet until pink disappears. Transfer to a large saucepan with a slotted spoon. Sauté onions and pepper in some of the fat left in skillet. Add to saucepan. Add tomatoes (cut into pieces), herbs and seasonings to saucepan and simmer for half an hour. Cut up half the cheese and add to the pan. Add marinara sauce.

Cook shells in boiling salted water, being careful not to overcook, and drain very well. Add shells to sauce, mix well; pour into a large shallow casserole dish or baking pan and top with remaining cheese (grated or sliced). Bake 1 hour at 350 °F uncovered. Allow to stand for 10 minutes before serving.

Shirley Verrett

An American soprano with a dramatic stage presence and voice whose large repertoire includes Sélika (*L'Africaine*), Dido (*Les Troyens*), Elisabetta (*Maria Stuarda*), both Adalgisa and Norma (*Norma*), Carmen and Amneris. She has appeared in the major opera houses of the world and gives regular recitals.

Hay and Straw

FOR 4–6 PEOPLE

6 oz yellow noodles (or spaghetti)
6 oz green noodles
boiling water, salt
3 tablespoons olive oil
1 clove garlic, halved

1 medium onion, chopped
¾ lb fresh mushrooms, sliced
¼ lb unsalted butter
black pepper to taste
¼ lb Parmesan cheese, grated

Cook yellow and green noodles in boiling water (in separate saucepans), each with ¾ teaspoon salt, half a tablespoon of olive oil, for the time specified on each package – usually 10 to 12 minutes. Drain the pasta, rinse in hot water, and keep hot.

Meanwhile, sauté garlic in 1 tablespoon oil for three minutes, and discard. Add to the oil the chopped onion and sauté until tender for about 5 minutes. Remove. Add the mushrooms to the remaining oil and sauté for 5 minutes or longer, stirring constantly.

Have ready a large earthenware, enamel or glass bowl containing the butter, which has been broken into 6 or 8 chunks. Add noodles, onions, and mushrooms and toss, as you would a salad, to mix. Add salt to taste, as well as black pepper, then add half the grated cheese and toss again to distribute thoroughly. Pass remaining cheese to be added as desired.

Other additions to Hay and Straw may be chopped drained anchovy fillets, halved pickled artichoke hearts, or olives (ripe, green or Greek style). In adding any of these, do not salt dish until they have been incorporated.

Salads, Vegetables
and Sauces

Carol Neblett

Potato Salad Inspired by the Tuscans

SERVES 8 NORMAL APPETITES OR 4 HUNGRY SINGERS OR 2 POTATO 'NUTS'

5 lbs unpeeled potatoes
8 yellow-skinned onions or soft flavoured English onions
2 large garlic cloves
1 large stalk fresh celery
4 raw eggs in their shells
2 whole green peppers
2 beef stock cubes
3–4 cups (1 pint) home-made mayonnaise
salt and pepper
dill (optional)

Cover the first 6 ingredients with water in a large pot and bring to a rapid boil. Add 2 beef stock cubes. Cook until potatoes are *al dente*. No mushy potatoes, please! Pour all the ingredients into a large colander and allow to cool. Now comes the tedious, but soon to be rewarded task of peeling potatoes, onions and eggs and cutting them all up into bite-sized pieces, not forgetting the green peppers which should be diced into the rest of the ingredients. Then mix in the mayonnaise very gently and add seasoned salt and ground white pepper, also dill weed if you desire. Serve cold.

Alberto Remedios

Chinese Salad

bean shoots
cucumber
green peppers
onion
celery
corn
tomato
salt and pepper
garlic

Mix the above ingredients in quantities and proportions according to your need and taste. Toss in a tasty French dressing using 1 part vinegar or lemon juice to 5 parts olive oil with seasonings to taste.

David Rendall

Ratatouille

FOR 4 PEOPLE

½lb aubergines
½lb courgettes
1 teaspoon salt
6 tablespoons olive oil
½lb thinly sliced onions
2 sliced green peppers
2 cloves mashed garlic
salt and pepper to taste
1 lb firm ripe red tomatoes
3 tablespoons finely chopped parsley

Peel the aubergines and cut them lengthwise into slices about ⅜ inch thick, about 2½–3 inches long and 1 inch wide. Scrub the courgettes and cut into slices about the same size as the aubergines. Place the vegetables in a bowl and toss with the salt. Let it stand for 30–40 minutes. Wash, drain and dry each slice in a cloth.

One layer at a time, sauté the aubergines and then the courgettes in some olive oil. Brown on each side very lightly. Remove to a side dish. In the same pan cook the onions and peppers slowly for 10 minutes or until tender but not browned. Add the garlic and salt and pepper to taste. The tomatoes must now be added, but first they must have their skins removed. This is best done by immersing into hot water and then peeling. Remove pips. Slice the tomatoes into ½ inch strips. Lay them over the onions and peppers. Season with salt and pepper. Cover the pan and cook over a low heat for 5 minutes or until tomatoes have begun to render their juice. Uncover, baste tomatoes with juices, raise heat and boil for several minutes until juice has almost evaporated.

Place ⅓ of tomato mixture (onions and peppers included) on base of casserole and sprinkle over 1 tablespoon parsley. Arrange over this ½ of the aubergines, then ½ of the courgettes and ½ of the remaining tomatoes and parsley. Repeat until all vegetables have been used. Cover the casserole and simmer over a low heat for 10 minutes. Uncover and baste with juices being careful not to mess up the layers. Add salt and pepper if necessary. Uncover and raise heat slightly and cook for a further 15 minutes. Be careful not to burn the bottom of the pan. Leave aside uncovered and serve at room temperature. This dish is better cooked a day prior to eating, as the flavour improves. It also freezes and is a treat indeed at Christmas as an unusual accompaniment to turkey.

Roderick Kennedy

Chinese Fried Rice with Mushrooms

FOR 2 PEOPLE

2 tablespoons oil
1 chopped onion
½lb button mushrooms
2 bowls cooked rice
1 tablespoon Soya sauce
salt and freshly ground pepper

Heat frying pan, add oil and chopped onion and fry until brown. Add coarsely chopped mushrooms and fry until semi-cooked. Add cold cooked rice and sauté gently until the whole begins to brown. Stir occasionally. When mixture is hot, add Soya sauce and season.

Riccardo Muti

One of the most gifted conductors performing today, he is currently Music Director of both the Philadelphia Orchestra and the Philharmonia Orchestra, London, in addition to being Principal Conductor of the Maggio Musicale, Florence. Known especially for being faithful to composers' original intentions, his refreshing interpretations of the popular Italian operas, in Florence, Vienna, Munich, Salzburg and London, have been balanced by reappraisals of neglected works, including *L'Africaine*, Spontini's *Agnes von Hohenstaufen* and an integral *Guillaume Tell*.

Gatto Napoletano

FOR 6 PEOPLE

2 lbs potatoes	2 eggs
salt and pepper	2 Mozzarella cheeses
pinch nutmeg	2 thick slices Mortadella
2 handfuls Parmesan cheese	1 handful breadcrumbs
1 glass milk	2 tablespoons olive oil

Boil the potatoes with skins on. Peel and make a purée. Add salt, pepper and nutmeg to taste, Parmesan cheese, milk and two eggs. Mix well and put a 1 inch layer into a well-oiled casserole. (In the meantime, heat the oven.) On top of this first layer put some slices of Mozzarella, slightly salted, and a sprinkling of Parmesan cheese. Put a second layer of purée and then some pieces of Mortadella along with another sprinkling of Parmesan cheese. Continue as above until ingredients are finished. On top put a layer of breadcrumbs and sprinkle oil over evenly. Cook in a medium oven for 20–25 minutes.

Leave to cool slightly before serving, so that the mixture is not too soft.

William Elvin

Cabbage Special (Vegetable Dish)

whole sliced cabbage (preferably white)
1 or 2 sliced carrots
3 tablespoons vegetable oil
4 tablespoons Soya sauce (preferably Japanese)
2 tablespoons sherry
5 tablespoons water

Sauté the vegetables in oil for approximately 5 minutes. Add the Soya sauce, sherry and water, close the lid and simmer until the vegetables get soft but not mushy.

Brigitte Fassbaender

This German-born mezzo-soprano, the daughter of baritone Willi Domgraf-Fassbaender, is one of the finest musicians singing today. She has sung in the opera houses of North America, Salzburg, Munich, Vienna, Milan and London in roles including Marina, Fricka, Dorabella, Carmen and Octavian. Her refined voice is also heard in excellent concerts and distinguished Lieder singing.

Hot Buttered Beets

Cook the beets (2–3 per person) for 15–20 minutes in a pressure cooker. Slice them and add to them fresh butter, salt and black pepper. Now cover with the sauce which is prepared by mixing the following ingredients together:

2 tablespoons yogurt
2 tablespoons mayonnaise
1 teaspoon caraway seeds
tarragon to season
a little vinegar
a little port wine
a pinch of garlic salt
2 small chillies, chopped

Anne Wilkens

Mushrooms à la Crème

(very good for topping steaks)

FOR 2 PEOPLE

2 oz butter
6 oz sliced mushrooms
salt and pepper
1 tablespoon brandy
4 tablespoons cream

Melt butter in frying pan, add mushrooms and lightly cook, season well. Pour in the brandy and set alight. When the flames have subsided, stir in the cream. Serve immediately.

Hildegard Heichele

Green Sauce

Chop very finely 2 handfuls of fresh herbs (chervil, parsley roots, chives or spring onions, borage, cress, tarragon, dandelion leaves, lovage, lemon balm, mint, etc.). Mix together 1 grated onion and 1 garlic clove, 2 finely chopped hard-boiled eggs and 1 cup of olive oil. Season to taste with wine vinegar or lemon juice, white pepper and salt. You may if you choose mix in 4 tablespoons mayonnaise or thick sour cream. Serve the sauce cooled.

John Dobson

An English-born member of The Royal Opera, London. He has a large and varied repertoire which consists of over sixty roles. He has performed over 1,200 times at Covent Garden and his character roles are noted for their wit and excellence and include Sellem in *The Rake's Progress*, Loge, Blind and Mime.

Red Tomato Chutney

A dozen miles to the north of Bakewell in the Peak District is some of the finest walking country in the British Isles, and what better lunch could one have after the long climb up Jacob's Ladder from Edale on to Kinder Scout than a thick sandwich of Derbyshire sage cheese with spicy tomato chutney!

40 tomatoes, skinned and chopped
12 oz sultanas
2 lbs brown sugar
6 tablespoons ground ginger
3 onions, sliced thinly or chopped
3 oz mustard seed
3 oz salt
4 teaspoons cayenne pepper
1½ pints vinegar

Put everything in a large saucepan and simmer for 3 hours or until thick. It can be started in a pressure cooker. Keeps very well and is nice and peppery. It should be poured whilst still hot into clean warmed jars, and either covered hot or left to cool thoroughly before covering.

Richard Van Allan

Raspberry or Blackberry Vinegar

Delicious on pancakes or on Yorkshire puddings (actually eaten as puddings!) or on ice-cream. When warmed and further sugar is added it is ideal for children suffering from heavy bronchial colds, helps to cut catarrh and give a good night's sleep!

6 lbs raspberries or blackberries
5 lbs caster sugar
3 pints white vinegar

Crush fruit with a wooden spoon. Mix with caster sugar. Add and mix vinegar. Cover bowl and contents and leave for 6 days. Strain liquid and using a wooden spoon work the pulp through a fine sieve so all seeds are removed. Heat over a low flame to ensure sugar is dissolved. Simmer syrup for 20 minutes. Bottle and cork while still hot.

The syrup can be diluted with water as required. If kept in a sealed container it will remain good for at least 20 years!

It is basically a sweet and sour syrup which can be used with many puddings.

Robin Leggate

This young English tenor has sung in operas and concerts throughout Great Britain. A member of The Royal Opera, he is a highly intelligent musician and his forte is the Mozartian and Italian repertoire. He has been heard in the roles of Tamino, Don Ottavio and Cassio, among others.

Home-made Yogurt

MAKES 2 PINTS YOGURT

2 pints milk
1 tablespoon live yogurt

Contrary to popular belief, it is very easy to make yogurt at home without the aid of expensive equipment. Home-made yogurt is far superior in taste to the bought variety and has many uses. I often eat it for breakfast with some runny honey, as it is eaten in Greece. It can also be used instead of cream on puddings, and where cream is called for in recipes yogurt is often as good and much cheaper!

Boil the milk for 5 minutes and let it cool to just above blood temperature (you can *just* hold your little finger in it). Then pour into a bowl and stir in a tablespoon of the last batch of yogurt. Your first batch will have to be made using plain yogurt bought from a shop.* Cover the bowl with a plate and a tea towel and stand on the central heating boiler or in the airing cupboard or in a similar warm place. Depending on the temperature it will set in 3–5 hours. As soon as it is set spoon off any clear liquid and put the yogurt in the fridge immediately. If it is left too long on the boiler it will go rather too sour.

Notwithstanding my original comment about expensive equipment, I have a milk saver, which stops the milk boiling over and a thermometer (which shows the required temperature to be about 125 °F). Both are useful but neither is essential.

---

* As a starter the shop-bought yogurt has either to be *very* fresh or else bought specifically as 'live' yogurt from a health food store.

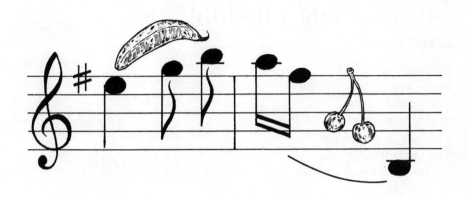

Puddings and Desserts

Josephine Veasey

Sussex Pond Pudding

FOR 3−4 PEOPLE

6 oz plain flour
pinch salt
3 oz grated suet
2 oz butter
2 oz soft brown sugar
3 oz currants
1 whole lemon to garnish

To form the suet pastry mix the first 3 ingredients together in the usual way. Line a 1 pint basin with ¾ of the dough. Place the remaining ingredients in the centre of the lined suet basin. Cover with the remaining dough and steam in a saucepan for 2 hours. Serve with a piece of lemon.

Marita Napier

Never Fails Apple Pie

FOR 6 PEOPLE

Crust
5 cups flour
1 lb shortening
1 egg
1 teaspoon salt
1 tablespoon vinegar
1 tablespoon brown sugar and water to make 1 cup

Mix flour and shortening, add egg, salt, then slowly add liquid.
Line dish with pastry, leave enough to top the pie. If dough is
too sticky, add more flour or chill for a short while.

Filling
2 lbs apples
½ cup sugar
2 tablespoons cinnamon
½ cup honey or syrup
pinch salt

Peel and slice apples, lay on pastry, mix sugar, cinnamon, honey
and salt, pour over apples and cover with remaining pastry.
Flute edges well, bake at 425 °F for about 45 min.
   This pie tastes best when served directly from the oven.
Cream is optional, as the pie has a lot of juice from the honey,
etc.

Elizabeth Connell

Born in South Africa, this mezzo-soprano is a member of English National Opera. She has sung extensively with the Welsh National Opera and at Covent Garden. Her roles in *War and Peace, Don Carlos, Luisa Miller* and *Bluebeard's Castle* have also often taken her abroad.

Liza's Apple Pie

FOR 4 PEOPLE

2 tablespoons butter
2 tablespoons sugar
2 tablespoons oil
1 large or 2 small eggs
2 teaspoons vanilla
2 cups flour
2 teaspoons baking powder
your own version of apple filling

Cream butter and sugar. Add oil and beat well. Beat eggs and add to mixture, then add vanilla. Sift together the flour and baking powder and add a little at a time. You may need a little more flour depending on the volume of the eggs. Work in well till the mixture comes away from the sides of the bowl. Knead for a few minutes. Divide the mixture and press one half into a buttered pie dish. Fill with your favourite pie filling. Sprinkle with sugar and spices. Then take the second half of the dough mixture and gently grate through the large holes on a grater so that the top of the pie is decorated with curls of pastry. Bake for half an hour at 350 °F. Delicious with cream or on its own.

Thomas Allen

A fine British baritone known for his many roles including the Count Almaviva, Papageno, Figaro and Billy Budd. He imbues his roles with character, imagination and a wonderful sense of humour. His voice is uniquely touching and he has great sympathy and communication with the audience. His roles are now taking him to all the world's opera houses.

Apple Gingerbread Surprise

FOR 2–3 PEOPLE

Topping:
2 dessert apples
2 oz butter
2 oz brown sugar

Cake:
4 oz self-raising flour
½ teaspoon salt
1½ teaspoons ginger
1 teaspoon grated nutmeg
4 oz butter
4 oz soft brown sugar
grated rind and juice of 1 lemon
2 eggs

Peel, core and slice apples. Cream together butter and sugar and spread over bottom and sides of 8 inch cake tin. Arrange apple slices evenly over base.

For the cake: sift flour, salt and spices together. Cream butter and sugar with lemon rind and juice. Beat in eggs. Fold in flour and spices. Spread mixture over apples. Bake in the middle of the oven at Gas Mark 4, 350 °F for 45 minutes. Serve hot or cold with cream.

Malcolm King

This English-born bass is now an Italian resident. He has sung throughout England, Scotland and Wales with all the leading British companies. His repertoire includes Leporello, Collatinus, Caspar and roles in *The Rake's Progress*, *Pelléas et Mélisande* and *We Come to the River*. He is known throughout Europe for his busy concert career and has recently appeared in the Losey film of *Don Giovanni*.

Tarte Tatin

FOR 2–4 PEOPLE

80 gm butter
80 gm sugar
a pinch of salt
1 egg
200 gm flour

Mix the butter (taken out of the refrigerator an hour ago) with the sugar and salt (with a *wooden* spoon, very important!) until it's perfectly homogenous. Add a whole egg and mix. Add the flour, mix and eventually make a compact ball of the lot and put it in the refrigerator for at least 30 minutes.

160 gm butter
160 gm sugar
1·5 kg crisp cooking apples
a good pinch of vanilla sugar

Start warming the oven to 375°, Mark 5. Put the butter in a flameproof dish 10 inches in diameter and 3 inches deep, over a hot plate. When it's warming, sprinkle with $\frac{2}{3}$ of the sugar, then add the apples (peeled and cut in thick pieces). Add the vanilla sugar to the rest of the sugar and sprinkle this mixture over the apples. Let it cook on a medium heat until you see caramel appearing between the apples. Roll the pastry on a little flour (to avoid its sticking to the table) with a rolling pin (or a clean bottle of Volvey!) to the required size. Skilfully transpose it over the dish, letting the edges fall inside the dish and pierce it all over with a fork. Put it into the oven. Keep an eye on it for 30 minutes (to be sure it doesn't burn), then cover with aluminium paper, turn down the heat and leave it in the oven for a further 10 minutes. Take the tarte out, place it on a wet piece of material for 10 minutes then back on to the hot plate for a minute before removing it swiftly from the dish. Voila!

Grace Bumbry

Sweet Potato Pie

FOR 4 PEOPLE

5 medium-sized sweet potatoes
1 cup (6 oz) sugar
1 cup (6 fl oz) milk
4 oz butter
1 teaspoon nutmeg
1 teaspoon lemon juice
a pinch baking soda
8 oz shortcrust pastry

Boil sweet potatoes until soft, then mash, making sure to remove all strings. Mix with sugar, milk, butter and nutmeg. Add lemon juice and baking soda. Pour mixture into pastry-lined flan case. Place in preheated oven at 375 °F and bake until brown (for about 40–50 minutes).

Lucia Popp

Plum Dumplings

(*Slivkové Gulky* in her native Slovak)

FOR 4–6 PEOPLE

400 gm unpeeled potatoes
150 gm flour
40 gm butter
1 egg
salt
1 kg Carlsbad plums
cottage cheese
100 gm butter for melting
120 gm icing sugar
sour cream

Boil the potatoes on the previous day, and then peel them after. Add flour, butter, egg and salt to potatoes. Work them into a smooth paste. Roll with a rolling pin on a floured wooden board. Cut into equal squares (6–8 cm). In each square put one

166

whole plum (leaving stone inside). Fold all corners of the square to the middle over the plum to completely surround it, and to form a round ball. Put the completed balls into boiling salted water which henceforth should simmer. Simmer for 5–7 minutes and then take them out and strain and place on a warm dish. Cover the hot dumplings with cottage cheese plus 100 gm melted butter (a lot!) and a lot of icing sugar topped finally with sour cream to taste. Serve hot. For those with a *very* sweet tooth there should be a separate dish of icing sugar!

Eva Randová

Damson Dumplings

FOR 4 PEOPLE

⅓ litre (275 ml) milk
semolina (about 100 gm)
1 egg
¾ kg damsons (or 100 gm dried apricots soaked and drained)

150 gm curd cheese
1 cup (60 ml) sour cream
75 gm caster sugar
50 gm butter, melted

Bring the milk to the boil and add the semolina until it becomes a firm dough. Allow the dough to cool somewhat, and then put it on a board and work the egg into it. So that the dough will not adhere to the hands or to the board, dust both with flour. Wrap dough and chill till cold. Now when the dough is ready it is rolled out 3–4 cm thick; press it flat and place the damsons side by side upon it. Cut off pieces around each damson, and bury it in the dough to make a dumpling. Place them in a pot in boiling salted water, and cook until all the dumplings are swimming on the surface of the water. The dumplings are served thus: lay the dumplings on a plate, cover them with curd cheese, then pour on sour cream, caster sugar and finally, hot butter. It should take 60 minutes. Cheers!

John Dobson

Bakewell Tart

MAKES 4–8 SLICES

'As a fervent Derbyshire man I am happy to choose a favourite recipe for Bakewell Tart. Bakewell is a delightful village nestling in the foothills of the Peak District and has for many, many years been famous for its Bakewell Tarts.'

6 oz shortcrust pastry
a little raspberry jam
lemon curd
2 oz butter
3 oz sugar
2 eggs
3 oz ground almonds
grated rind and juice of 1 lemon
3 oz Madeira cake crumbs

Line a sponge tin with the pastry and spread with jam and lemon curd. Cream the butter and sugar, add the well-beaten eggs, ground almonds, lemon rind, cake crumbs and lemon juice. Pour on to the jam in the dish and bake in a moderately hot oven for about 30–40 minutes.

Josef Meinrad

A great Austrian actor who is a member of the Burghtheater, Vienna, where he has appeared in many of the Russian, English and German classics. He has appeared in many musicals and his link with opera is his famous interpretation of Frosch in *Die Fledermaus*, which is well known at the Vienna State Opera and The Royal Opera, London.

Curd Strudel

MAKES 8 PIECES

To make the dough take 100 gm plain flour, a sprinkle of oil and a sprinkle of warm water (about 1 tablespoon of each). Mix and knead together till the dough no longer clings to the hands. Leave for 10 minutes under a warm dish. Sprinkle a cloth with flour. Draw out the dough as thin as possible (until it almost breaks up). Cut off the thick edges.

Filling
250 gm curds (medium fat curd cheese)
1 egg yolk
3 tablespoons sugar
1 grated lemon rind
vanilla sugar

Beat up the above ingredients into a cream and spread over the flat dough. Using the cloth, roll up the dough, spreading with butter as it is rolled then close the two ends of the strudel by pinching the edges of the dough together. Spread a tin plate with butter, place strudel on it and bake in the oven for 20–25 minutes at a medium temperature.

Karl Böhm

One of the world's great conductors, Karl Böhm was born in
Austria and is well known for his performances with the world's
top orchestras, and particularly for his sensitive interpretations
of Mozart's music. He has conducted major orchestras of North
America and Europe and is the lifetime Honorary Conductor of
his native Vienna Philharmonic. He is also an honorary citizen of
both Graz and Salzburg. A friend of Richard Strauss, he has
championed his music since his pre-war days at the Dresden
State Opera. He has conducted an operatic repertoire of over 160
operas in all the major opera houses of the world and is much
honoured for his great services to music.

Curd Strudel à la Cilly (Curd Cheese Strudel)

For many years Cilly Hahnkamper has been a valuable member of the Böhm household in Vienna and responsible for the preparation of all the celebrated conductor's meals. Anyone who has had the good fortune to be entertained at the Böhms' house will not forget Cilly's talents. The conductor is of the opinion that they would grace any gourmet haunt, even in France. To celebrate her revered master's eightieth birthday Cilly announced to the *Salzburg Journal* that she had prepared one of his favourite dishes, Curd Cheese Strudel. Although it is not her normal practice to reveal her recipes, she does so here. Cilly's Curd Strudel, by the way, is quite a safe dish for anyone who is dieting.

Take ½kg 20% curds (low fat curd cheese), press out all the liquid, add an egg, some milk, a packet of vanilla sugar, and plain sugar to taste. Stir the whole well, and mix into a dough. Prepare raisins and shelled and chopped almonds. Spread a little butter over the rolled-out strudel dough, spread the raisins and almonds over it, and roll it up. Put it in a greased baking tin, smear butter lightly over it and bake at a moderate temperature.

'You can easily warm up the strudel,' says Cilly. 'You put some milk in an ovenproof dish, lay the strudel in it and warm it over a low heat.'

Norman Bailey

An English baritone whose operatic training took place mainly in Rhodesia. He is known particularly for his interpretations of Wagnerian roles, and has appeared in many major opera houses, festivals and on television. He is also identified with the roles of Jochanaan in *Salome*, Orestes in *Elektra* and the title role of *Macbeth*.

Koeksister Recipe (from South Africa)

FOR 6–8 PEOPLE

4 cups (1 lb 8 oz) plain flour
1 small level teaspoon salt
4 level teaspoons baking powder
4 tablespoons (4 ozs) butter
2 eggs
1 cup (6 fl oz) water

Sift flour and dry ingredients together, and then rub in the butter well. Beat the eggs; add water; mix with the dry ingredients to a soft dough. Roll out the dough to about $\frac{1}{4}$ inch thick. Cut long, narrow strips and plait these. Cut plaits into $2\frac{1}{2}$ inch lengths.

Heat oil for deep frying and fry *koeksisters* for about 2–3 minutes. Lift out of oil, drain, and dip immediately into ice-cold syrup. Lift out of syrup and drain.

Syrup
6 cups (2 lb 4 oz) sugar
3 cups (18 fl oz) water
$\frac{1}{2}$ teaspoon cream of tartar
$\frac{1}{2}$ teaspoon tartaric acid
Boil all the ingredients together for 10 minutes and allow to cool.

Comments: Full of calories but utterly delicious!

These are often served at the South African Braai-vleis (barbecue) and recall memories of marvellous evenings outdoors.

Evgeny Nesterenko

Blinis (Pancakes)

MAKES ABOUT 20 PANCAKES

1 lb 8 oz buckwheat or plain flour
1 oz fresh yeast or 2 level tablespoons dried yeast
2 cups (12 fl oz) tepid water
2 eggs, separated
2 tablespoons sugar
3 tablespoons butter, melted
1½ teaspoons salt
1 pint warm milk

Sift 1 lb of the flour into a bowl and cream the yeast with a little of the water. When smooth, add the rest of the water and pour into the flour. Mix to a dough using more flour if required. Knead until dough shines – for about 5 minutes. Place in a greased bowl, cover and leave until double in size.

Beat in the egg yolks, sugar, butter and salt. Mix in the remaining flour, knead until smooth. Gradually beat in the warm milk until dough becomes a batter. Allow to rise, knock back and repeat twice, covering on each occasion.

On the last rise, stiffly beat the egg whites and fold into the batter. Pour small quantities into a hot pan containing a little oil to make pancakes. Use instantly once the egg whites have been added.

NB Buckwheat flour is very hard to buy in England.

David Atherton

A young British conductor who has led all the major British orchestras and was co-founder of the London Sinfonietta with which he has premièred many works. In 1968 he became the youngest conductor to have worked with The Royal Opera. His repertoire includes *Carmen, Peter Grimes, Tosca* and *We Come to the River*. Recently appointed Principal Conductor of the Royal Liverpool Philharmonic Orchestra, he has travelled world-wide and is also well known for his writing on music.

Grand Marnier Pancakes

FOR 6 PEOPLE (2 PANCAKES EACH)

Batter
4 oz plain flour
½ teaspoon salt
1 egg
1 egg yolk
½ pint milk
tablespoon cooking oil

Sauce
2 oz butter
4 oz sugar
juice of 2 oranges
juice of 1 lemon
1 wineglass Grand Marnier

Sift flour and salt into a mixing bowl. Add the egg, egg yolk and half the milk. Mix together with a wooden spoon, then beat well making a smooth batter. Add the remaining ¼ pint milk and the oil. Put mixture into a jug to facilitate the pouring out of the batter. Heat a frying pan adding a small amount of oil or butter. Pour out pancake batter and cook, turning the finished pancake on to a plate.

For the sauce, melt some butter in a frying pan, stir in the sugar cooking slowly until it turns a golden brown caramel. Add orange and lemon juice (strained). Keep the pan bubbling hot until the caramel dissolves making a thick sauce. Place each flat pancake into the pan with the sauce one after the other, folding them into quarters and putting them on the side of the pan. When all the pancakes have been added pour Grand Marnier into the pan and flambé. Serve hot with sauce from pan.

Hildegard Heichele

Raspberry Crêpes

FOR 2−4 PEOPLE

Stir 2 fresh eggs, 4 rounded tablespoons wheaten flour, 1 cup (6 fl oz) lukewarm milk, 1 tablespoon raspberry essence and a pinch of salt to a fluid paste. Leave for 30 minutes. Cook 4 thin egg-cakes (pancakes) in a pan in hot fat until they are golden yellow on both sides. Then put 8 oz fresh raspberries on them. Sprinkle over them sugar, cinnamon and 2 oz flaked almonds. Serve on a previously warmed plate. When serving, pour on a glass of raspberry brandy or brandy or fruit liqueur, set it alight and leave it to flame. Sprinkle with caster sugar.

Elizabeth Bainbridge

Orange or Lemon Whip

FOR 4 PEOPLE

3 eggs
1 dessertspoon powdered gelatine
1 tablespoon cold water
5–6 oz caster sugar
grated rind of lemon or orange
5 tablespoons orange or lemon juice

Separate the yolks from the whites of the eggs. Soak the gelatine in the cold water. Beat the yolks with the sugar until light and creamy, add the orange or lemon rind and the juice.

Pour 2 tablespoons boiling water on to the gelatine. Stir until dissolved, cool and add to the egg mixture. Mix thoroughly, and when nearly set slowly fold in stiffly beaten egg whites. Turn into a bowl to set.

David Ward

This Scottish-born bass, now retired to New Zealand, was
known for his Wagnerian and Verdi roles, particularly Wotan,
Philip II, Fiesco, and Rocco. He was a member of The Royal
Opera Company at Covent Garden, and many guest
appearances took him to North and South America, the United
States and throughout Europe.

Orange and Lemon Soufflé

FOR 6–8 PEOPLE

strained juice of 4 oranges
1 envelope gelatine
6 eggs, separated
grated rind of 1 lemon and 1 orange
1 cup (6 oz) sugar
strained juice of 1½ lemons
¼ teaspoon salt
2 cups heavy cream (12 fl oz double cream)

Pour ½ cup of orange juice into small dish, sprinkle with gelatine
and leave for at least 5 minutes. Place egg yolks in a heavy
saucepan. Add rinds, sugar, remaining orange juice, lemon juice
and salt. Beat with an electric beater until thick and creamy.
Place over a low heat and cook, stirring constantly, until
mixture coats spoon. Take off heat and pour in gelatine mixture
stirring till completely dissolved. Cool for about 20 minutes.
Beat whites until they are stiff. Whip cream. Combine, fold both
into orange mixture. Best left in refrigerator for several hours or
made the day before.

Lillian Watson

An English soprano who has sung primarily with British opera companies in such roles as Zerlina, Papageno, Susanna, Despina and Barbarina. She also appears regularly in concerts, recitals and television broadcasts.

Lemon Cream Torte

FOR 6–8 PEOPLE

1 cup crushed sweet biscuits
½ teaspoon cinnamon
½ teaspoon nutmeg
2 oz melted butter
¾ cup fresh lemon juice
finely grated rind of 1 lemon and 1 orange
1 tin condensed milk
½ pint double cream

Mix first 4 ingredients together thoroughly and press down firmly into an 8 inch flan dish. Bake in a moderate oven for 10 minutes and allow to cool. Mix lemon juice, rind and condensed milk together and allow to stand for 15 minutes. Whip cream stiffly and fold into lemon mixture. Pile on to biscuit base and refrigerate, serve cold.

Hildegard Heichele

Cheese Flan (Cheesecake)

FOR 6–8 PEOPLE

Beat 100 gm butter, 5 egg yolks and 350 gm sugar to a froth.
Take 50 gm coarsely chopped almonds, the juice and rind of 1
lemon, 500–750 gm curds (medium fat curd cheese) dried as
much as possible and 5 or 6 tablespoons semolina. Beat up the
whole and add the whites of the eggs very firmly beaten. Bake
in a baking tin (9 inch square) for about 1 hour at medium
temperature (Gas Mark 5, 375 °F, 180 °C).
Important: Serve hot.

Anne Pashley

Chocolate Mousse de Pluckerett

FOR 6–8 PEOPLE

½ lb plain chocolate
2 tablespoons sweet sherry
1–2 tablespoons black coffee
6 eggs

Break up the chocolate and melt slowly over a very low flame
with the sherry and coffee. Separate eggs, add yolks to the
melted chocolate. (Remove stringy bits from yolks.) Stir till
uniform consistency and remove from flame. Turn into a bowl
and fold in the stiffly beaten egg whites. Cool and put in fridge
for an hour. Serve with whipped cream or just as it comes.
Particularly good with coffee.

Tom McDonnell

An Australian-born baritone whose appearances have been primarily in England and Australia in such roles as Count Almaviva, Escamillo, Prince Andrei and Papageno. He created leading roles in Ian Hamilton's *The Royal Hunt of the Sun* and Tippett's *The Ice Break*.

Capriccio au Chocolat

FOR 4–6 PEOPLE

'Guest performances in the kitchen only. Brief but triumphant forays, when from a fairly harmless Dr Jekyll, I become the gourmet Mr Hyde; tantrums, meticulous almost pedantic attention to detail and ingredients, (much to the irritation of my wife, a superb though intuitive cook), and smug satisfaction as "things" emerge swollen and created from my ovens. Three dinner guests fainted (with delight) after my world première of *Capriccio au Chocolat*, which I shall attempt to describe':

4 oz butter
6 oz bitter chocolate
2 tablespoons flour
¾ lb caster sugar
4 eggs, separated
3 oz ground almonds
3 tablespoons brandy

Melt the butter and chocolate carefully in the oven. Mix it with the flour, sugar, beaten egg yolks, almonds and brandy. Fold in the stiffly beaten whites, a process of some grace and delicacy. Turn into a buttered cake tin and cook in a preheated oven, Gas Mark 4, 355 °F, for 35 minutes. There will be a thin crust on top of the cake, and inside, it will be rather softer, which is just right as it firms as it cools. When cool, cover the cake with whipped cream (adding a teaspoon of brandy).

Anne Wilkens

An English mezzo–soprano, for some years a member of The Royal Opera, she makes frequent guest appearances with the major British companies. Her many roles include Kate Pinkerton, Laura, Maddalena and Olga.

Choc-Orange Cups

FOR 4 PEOPLE

4 oz plain chocolate
2 eggs, separated
1 small can mandarin oranges
¼ pint double cream
1 chocolate flake bar
orange liqueur (optional)

Slowly melt plain chocolate in a bowl over hot water. Whisk the egg whites very stiffly. When chocolate has melted, stir in the two egg yolks, then fold in the whisked whites. Divide the chocolate mixture between four little dishes. Arrange a few orange segments on top of each one, and top with a thick layer of whipped cream. Decorate with orange segments and crumbled chocolate flake. A tablespoon of orange liqueur added with the egg yolks makes it even better!

Eva Turner

Russian Pudding

FOR 4 PEOPLE

4 oz butter
4 oz caster sugar
4 oz ground almonds
4 oz Madeira cake
2 egg yolks
2 tablespoons sherry
strawberry jam
1 packet Boudoir biscuits
whipped cream to decorate

Cream well together the butter and sugar. In another bowl mix
together the ground almonds and the cake (finely crumbed).
Add to this one egg yolk and one tablespoon of sherry and
blend, then add the second egg yolk and the second tablespoon
of sherry. Mix this well together, to form a thick mixture and

add to this the creamed butter and sugar. Make sure that the whole is well integrated. Take a 1½–2 pint pudding basin and into the bottom put a good tablespoon of strawberry jam (mash up any whole fruit). Spread the jam halfway up the side of the basin, then line with the Boudoir biscuits. Into this press well the above mixture quite tightly, cover the top with a circle of greaseproof paper or foil and put a small weight on top. For the fullest flavour prepare at least 24 hours before required and keep in the refrigerator.

To serve, run a knife round and turn out on to a flat dish so that the jam end is uppermost. Decorate with whipped cream but allow some of the jam to show through. Cut portions with a knife, like you would a gâteau.

Kate Gielgud

Rich Easy Trifle

FOR 4–6 PEOPLE

'A trifle can be made with convenience foods that can be very impressive (tasty anyway!).'

1 packet raspberry jam Swiss roll
2 or more tablespoons sherry
raspberries, fresh, frozen, or tinned
4 oz walnuts
1 packet coffee 'Angel Delight' or any other flavour
8 oz whipping cream

Arrange the sliced Swiss roll in the bottom of a medium-sized deep dish. Sprinkle with sherry and any raspberry juice. Place raspberries on top and cover with walnuts reserving about 8 halves for decoration. Make up the coffee whip according to instructions and spoon over raspberries and walnuts. Top with whipped cream and decorate with walnut halves.

Tom McDonnell

Ecstase d'Anita

'I must not allow myself to dwell on the title, but rather proceed to the ingredients':

FOR 6–8 PEOPLE

8 oz unsalted butter
6 oz caster sugar
6 oz ground almonds
3 egg yolks ⎤ lightly whisked
2 tablespoons double cream ⎦ together
4 tablespoons brandy
50 sponge fingers
½ pint cold strong black coffee
sprinkling of blanched almonds

Cream the butter and sugar. Stir in ground almonds, alternating with the lightly whisked egg and cream mixture. Add the brandy a few drops at a time, stirring carefully to avoid curdling. Quickly dip each sponge finger into the coffee without allowing it to soak and gently smooth some of the butter mixture along one side. Repeating this process, arrange 25 sponge fingers, butter to biscuit, on a longish dish. Do the same for the second layer, buttering one side of each biscuit and placing them on top of the first layer. Smooth gently using a broad-bladed knife. Garnish with almonds. Chill for 12 hours or more.

Vassile Moldoveanu

A Romanian tenor, originally the Principal Tenor of the
Romanian National Opera. He has now sung with most major
opera companies in Europe and North America. His repertoire
includes the roles of Don Carlos, Pinkerton, Tamino and Don
Ottavio.

Champagne Biscuit Flan with Walnut Cream

'Cooking is my favourite hobby. In the morning, after a glass of
fresh fruit juice, I like to prepare myself a full breakfast with
fried eggs and bacon, cheese, bread and butter and milk. At
mid-day I like a meal of lean veal, beef or chicken, with a light
sauce. Most of all I like a well-seasoned grilled steak, with
mashed potatoes and plenty of mixed raw vegetable salad. For
dessert I like walnut pudding, or occasionally a Champagne
Biscuit Flan with Walnut Cream, which can be prepared cold,
and I give you the recipe for it herewith.'

250 gm butter
250 gm sugar
4 eggs, separated
300 gm ground walnuts
2 packets vanilla sugar
½ kg cold milk
500 gm Champagne biscuits (spoon biscuits or Boudoir biscuits)

Stir the butter and sugar together so that the sugar is well
blended in the butter, all the time adding the egg yolks. Then
mix into it the ground walnuts, while adding the egg whites
which have been beaten up into a froth. Then, having dissolved
the vanilla sugar in the cold milk, quickly soak the spoon
biscuits in it, and lay out a row of them on a plate. Cover these
with the creamy paste and lay the next row of biscuits over it.
When you have four rows, cover with the paste on the top and
the sides of the flan. In order to make the flan firm keep it for a
while in the refrigerator.

185

Yvonne Minton

The Australian mezzo-soprano whose dramatic acting and beautiful voice are known to opera lovers throughout the world. She is often seen in roles such as Dorabella, Cherubino, Octavian, Olga, Dido, Kundry, Waltraute and Brangäne.

Classic Pavlova

FOR 4−6 PEOPLE

3 egg whites (should be at room temperature)
pinch of salt
$\frac{3}{4}$ cup (6 oz) caster sugar
$\frac{1}{4}$ cup (6 oz) granulated sugar
1 tablespoon cornflour
1 teaspoon lemon juice
fruit and cream to serve

Beat egg whites and salt until stiff and dry. Add caster sugar gradually (a dessertspoon at a time) beating well between each addition. Make sure that the sugar is completely dissolved. Mix together granulated sugar and cornflour and lightly fold into egg white mixture together with lemon juice. Spread on a Pavlova plate bringing the sides up and swirling to make a shell. Bake in a very slow oven, electric 30–40 minutes, gas 1 hour or until Pavlova is dry to touch. Allow to cool in the oven. To serve whip fresh cream and fill Pavlova shell with it. Decorate with strawberries, passion fruit, bananas or Kiwi fruit.

Alberto Remedios

Pavlova

FOR 6–8 PEOPLE

4 egg whites (preferably 5)
225 gm (8 oz) caster sugar
20 ml (4 level teaspoons) cornflour
10 ml (2 teaspoons) vanilla essence
284 ml (½ pint) double cream
2–3 passion fruit
350 gm (12 oz) raspberries or bananas

To line tin or round baking tray use special non-stick vegetable parchment or tin foil brushed with corn oil.

Whisk the egg whites until stiff. Whisk in half of the sugar gradually then whisk in the remaining sugar with the cornflour and vanilla essence. Pile on to the non-stick paper and bake at 140 °C (275 °F, Gas Mark 1) for about 1¼ hours. When cool turn out on to a plate and top with filling (cream, passion fruit, raspberries or banana or own choice).

Paul Hudson

Slimmers' Sweet

TO SERVE 6 SOPRANOS OR 2 BASSES:

2 cartons plain yogurt
8 oz can purée marrons glacés
8 oz can apricots, drained and puréed
¼ pint double cream, whipped

Gently fold together all ingredients, chill and serve with ratafia biscuits or miniature meringues.

Unfortunately, I cannot claim to be the originator of either of my recipes, but both dishes were specially prepared for me by Irene Canning, the proprietor and chef extraordinaire of Gibson's Restaurant, in Cardiff, knowing my love of game and dislike of heavy sweets.

John Pritchard

Cold Gooseberry Pudding

FOR 4 PEOPLE

Top and tail 1 lb gooseberries. Smear over bottom and sides of soufflé dish (JP's is 8 inches in diameter) 3 oz butter then put in the bottom 3 oz brown sugar and 2 oz chopped walnuts. Add the gooseberries.

Mix together ¼ lb each self-raising flour, butter and granulated sugar. Add two eggs. Spread this sponge mixture over gooseberries and bake in a medium oven for approximately one hour or until pudding leaves sides of dish and is cooked in the centre. Leave to cool before turning out, but it is best to turn it out rather than keep in dish otherwise it might stick to the bottom. Serve with plenty of fresh cream.

Peter Maag

Fragole Meyerbeer (Strawberries à la Meyerbeer)

FOR 4 PEOPLE

500 gm strawberries
1 glass liquid cream
½ cup sugar
black pepper (ground at last moment!)
1 glass Cointreau

Cut the strawberries into 4 parts, cover with cream, sugar and black pepper, pour glass of Cointreau over mixture and stir.

Lamberto Gardelli

An Italian-born conductor who now lives in England. He regularly appears with most of the major opera houses in Scandinavia, Italy, the United States, Budapest and at Covent Garden. He is particularly known for his idiomatic interpretations of his native Italian operatic repertoire, including recent recordings of early Verdi operas which have done much to re-establish these works throughout the world.

Banana Dream

FOR 2–4 PEOPLE

4 bananas
50 gm butter
1 tablespoon sugar
50 gm chopped almonds
½ litre vanilla ice-cream (home-made or not)
50 gm bitter chocolate

Cut the bananas lengthwise and in the middle. Heat the butter in a saucepan and lay the bananas with care in the nearly brown butter. Spread the sugar over and fry 3–4 minutes on each side. Put the bananas in a flat bowl and let them cool off. Spread over the chopped almonds and then put the ice-cream cut into slices on top. Cover with chopped bitter chocolate and put in the fridge for about an hour. The ice-cream will be soft and funnily enough, nobody can guess what is underneath.

Donald McIntyre

Pineapple Delight

FOR 2–4 PEOPLE

(very quick and easy, any tinned fruits can be used)

1 jar plain yogurt
1 tin crushed pineapple
1 cup brown breadcrumbs and ½ cup demarara sugar mixed together
½ pint whipped cream
decoration: chopped nuts etc. as desired

Arrange 2 layers each of yogurt, fruit, breadcrumbs and sugar mixture and cream in glass dishes. Decorate to taste with chopped nuts, fruit, cream etc. Chill in fridge. Must be served soon after making or the sugar mixture is no longer crunchy.

Carlo Bergonzi

Cheer-me-up Pudding (Tirami su')

FOR 10 PEOPLE

10 egg yolks
20 tablespoons of dry marsala wine
10 tablespoons sugar
2 tablespoons dry white wine
2 tablespoons water
3 tablespoons brandy
½kg mascarpone (type of cream cheese)
Savoiardi biscuits, as many as are required (Boudoir biscuits)
6 coffeecups bitter coffee
grated chocolate

In a bain marie make a zabaglione using the 10 egg yolks, the marsala and the sugar, white wine, water and brandy over a low flame. Whisk the mixture until thick and frothy.

When the mixture is cool, add sieved mascarpone. Dip biscuits into coffee. Take a mould, start with a layer of the cream mixture, then a layer of biscuits, continue until mixture is used up. Sprinkle top with grated chocolate and put into refrigerator.

Lamberto Gardelli

Light Ice-cream

FOR 4–6 PEOPLE

4 eggs
4 tablespoons icing sugar
50 gm chopped chocolate
50 gm chopped walnuts
400 ml whipping cream

Separate the whites from the yolks. Whip the yolks with the sugar, add chocolate and walnuts or your choice of filling (also a drop of brandy is not a bad idea, just a teaspoon or two), then whip the cream as stiff as possible without making it like butter. Lastly, whip whites till stiff. Add the whipped cream to the yolks then the whites carefully. Put into an aluminium mould in the freezer for 2 hours, or into the fridge for 3–4. The use of the whites as well makes this ice-cream lighter and it goes well with any kind of fresh fruit.

Roderick Kennedy

Fruit Salad

Roderick Kennedy's suggestion for a pudding is a fruit salad sweetened with 6 oz caster sugar plus 2 tablespoons brandy and/or Cointreau and cream.

David Rendall

Instead of Dessert why not try a selection of
French blue cheeses:

Roquefort
Bleu de Bresse
Saingorlon
Bleu des Causses
Bleu de L'Aveyron

These are delicious without biscuits and butter but a little dry
French bread would not go amiss.

Blue cheese should be accompanied by a good red wine. St
Emilion or St Estephe: 1964, 66, 71 and 76 are very good
vintages.

Breads, Cakes
and Biscuits

Valerie Masterson

An attractive British soprano whose many roles include Countess Almaviva, Manon, Violetta, Micaëla and Marguérite. After a period with the D'Oyly Carte Company, she became a member of English National Opera, where she sung her first performances of most of the roles for which she has become well known. Her engagements have often taken her abroad, particularly to France; she makes regular appearances with the Paris Opéra and at the Aix-en-Provence Festival and is beloved by French audiences.

Bran Bread

MAKES A I LB LOAF

This dough keeps well in the deep freeze and can be made into rolls which can be heated straight from the freezer in the oven for unexpected guests.

2 oz bran
12 oz Millstone 81% plain compost flour
1 level teaspoon salt
1 level teaspoon sugar
½ oz margarine or cooking oil
½ oz fresh yeast (or 1 level tablespoon dried yeast)
8 oz tepid water

Place bran, flour, salt and sugar in a mixing bowl and rub in margarine. Stir yeast and water together until well blended. Add water to flour and mix well to form a manageable dough. Knead for 10 minutes. Fold dough into 3 and place in a well greased baking tin. Cover and leave to rise until double in size. Bake immediately for 30–40 minutes at 425 °F (Gas Mark 7–8).

Gwynne Howell

Bran Fruit Loaf

MAKES A 2 LB LOAF

125 gm (4 oz) natural wheat bran
150 gm (5 oz) caster sugar
275 gm (10 oz) mixed dried fruit
300 ml (½ pint) milk
125 gm (4 oz) self-raising flour

Place natural bran, sugar and dried fruit into a basin and mix
them well together. Stir in milk and leave to stand for half an
hour. Sieve in the flour, mixing well and pour mixture into
well-greased 2 lb loaf tin. Bake in a moderate oven at 180 °C
(350 °F, Gas Mark 4), for about 1 hour. Turn out of tin and
allow to cool. Cut into slices and spread with butter and honey.

Robert Tear

Bara Brith (Welsh Tea Bread)

12 oz mixed dried fruit
6 oz brown sugar
½ pint water
3 oz butter
1 egg
½ teaspoon mixed spice
12 oz self-raising flour

Simmer fruit, sugar, water, butter for ten minutes. When cool, add egg, spice, flour. Cook for 1½–1¾ hours in a 7–8 inch square tin at Gas Mark 2 (300 °F). Slice and butter.

Norma Burrowes

Cinnamon Bread

MAKES 2 1 LB LOAVES

4 oz butter or margarine
½ pint milk
1 oz fresh or dry yeast equivalent
6 oz sugar
pinch salt
1 egg
1 lb 4 oz flour
Filling
4 oz butter
2 oz sugar
3 tablespoons cinnamon
2 oz chopped almonds
2 oz currants or raisins

Melt the fat and add the milk. Dissolve the yeast (if dry in 1 teaspoon warm water, if fresh add a little sugar). Mix all ingredients into the flour. Leave to rise until double the size, then knead the dough, if necessary adding more flour. Roll out to a big square cake ½ inch thick. Cut into 2 inch pieces. Put in 2 1 lb loaf tins and leave to rise again. Brush with beaten egg and bake in the oven at 430 °F until golden brown (25 minutes).

To make the filling, mix butter, sugar and cinnamon together and then add the rest of the ingredients.

Alberto Remedios

Banana Bread

MAKES A I LB LOAF

½ cup (3 oz) butter
I cup (6 oz) sugar
2 eggs
2 cups (12 oz) plain flour
I level teaspoon baking powder
I level teaspoon baking soda
¼ teaspoon salt
3 very ripe bananas, mashed

Heat oven to 350 °F. Cream butter with sugar until light. Beat in the eggs. Sift together the flour, baking powder, baking soda and salt. Fold the bananas into the mixture and stir in the flour. Turn into an 8 inch greased loaf tin and bake for 45 minutes–1 hour until bread springs back when pressed in the centre.

Richard Cassilly

Carrot Cake

2 cups (12 oz) plain flour
2 teaspoons baking powder
1½ teaspoons baking soda
1 teaspoon salt
2 teaspoons cinnamon
2 cups (12 oz) sugar
1½ cups (9 fl oz) vegetable oil
4 eggs, beaten
2 cups (6 oz) finely grated carrots
1 8 oz can crushed pineapple, drained
½ cup (3 oz) chopped walnuts

Icing
8 oz cream cheese
8 oz icing sugar
vanilla essence

Sift dry ingredients together, add the rest and mix well. Place in greased and floured 13 ×9 inch cake tin and bake at 350 °F for about 1 hour. If cake is not quite cooked, lower heat to 325 °F and bake until cake is firm to touch.

Blend together the icing ingredients and use the mixture to top the cake when it is cool.

Carlo Bergonzi

Carrot Cake (Torta de Carote)

400 gm carrots
400 gm almonds
400 gm sugar
4 eggs, separated
1 portion pane degli angeli (a type of sweet Italian yeast)

Grate carrots, press firmly to remove water. Chop almonds or put in blender, so they are very thinly sliced. Melt sugar with egg yolks, beat well, then add carrots and almonds. Beat egg whites until very firm. Add yeast. Put mixture in cake tin, place in medium-low oven for 45 minutes.

Elizabeth Robson

Cheesecake

FOR 6–8 PEOPLE

Base
½lb plain chocolate digestive biscuits
3 oz butter or margarine
nutmeg or cinnamon

Filling
8 oz Philadelphia cream cheese
3 oz caster sugar
1 teaspoon vanilla essence
juice and zest of 1 lemon
2 eggs, separated
½ pint whipping cream
½oz gelatine
water
chocolate flake bar to decorate

Crush biscuits with a rolling pin (best done inside a strong polythene bag). Melt the butter with the spices and combine with the biscuits. The chocolate coating on the biscuits will also melt. Line the base of a 10 inch loose-bottomed cake tin with the biscuit mixture and leave to set.

Cream the cheese with sugar, vanilla and zest of lemon. Add egg yolks and lemon juice. Whip cream until it forms a continuous line from the back of a spoon like a piece of ribbon, and fold into cheese mixture. Make up the gelatine (twice as much water to gelatine) and leave the paste to stand while you whisk the egg whites. Fold egg whites into cheese mixture with a metal spoon, making as few folds as possible in order to keep the fluffiness. Heat gelatine gently and when dissolved thoroughly allow to cool before folding into the mixture. Pour this mixture into the base and leave to set for at least 2 hours. Decorate with grated chocolate (Cadbury's chocolate flake is excellent). This will keep for 4 days in the fridge and it freezes very well.

Thomas Allen

Banana and Walnut Cake

MAKES A 2 LB LOAF

1½ oz butter
1½ oz lard
4 oz caster sugar
1 beaten egg
grated zest of 1 lemon and 1 orange
8 oz plain flour
2 level teaspoons baking powder
4 medium-sized bananas
2 oz shelled walnuts

Preheat oven to Gas Mark 4 (350 °F). Cream fats together and add sugar. Beat until you have a consistency that drops easily off the spoon. Beat in the beaten egg, a teaspoon at a time, with continuous beating. Add lemon and orange zest. Sift flour and baking powder together, then fold with a metal spoon into mixture. Mash bananas in a basin with a large fork. Add to the mixture with the walnuts. Put into a buttered 2 lb loaf tin, level off. Bake in centre of the oven for 50–60 minutes. Cool and serve, sliced and buttered.

Carlo Bergonzi

Sweet Almond Cake

400 gm butter
400 gm sugar
500 gm ground almonds
400 gm plain flour
4 egg yolks

Cream butter and sugar. Work in almonds, flour and yolks.
Shape into a round. Cook for thirty minutes in a medium oven.

Ileana Cotrubas

Schwarzwälder Kirschtorte

(Blackforest Cake)

150 gm (5¼ oz) butter
150 gm (5¼ oz) sugar
2 small bags vanilla sugar (25 gm bags or 200 gm (7 oz) sugar and 1
   teaspoon vanilla essence)
6 eggs
110 gm (4 oz) ground almonds
150 gm (5¼ oz) plain chocolate, freshly grated
75 gm (3¼ oz) flour
75 gm (2¾ oz) cornflour (cornstarch)
3 level teaspoons baking powder
500 gm (17½ oz) pitted Morello cherries (these are the only
   recommended cherries; they are grown and imported in jars from
   Austria, Germany, Hungary, Poland, etc.)
0.3–0.5 l (11–17 fl oz) whipping cream
chocolate to decorate

Cream the butter and sugar, add the eggs and beat the mixture.
Add ground almonds and grated chocolate; add the flour and the
cornflour by degrees. Cook in a round 8–9 inch cake tin for one
hour at 200 °C (375–400 °F).

When it has cooled cut into 2 or 3 layers as you would for a
sandwich sponge cake. Soak first layer in the cherry juice and
spread with whipped cream and cherries. Cover with second
layer and soak and spread as before. The top layer should be
soaked again, but spread only with cream. Decorate with
cherries, chocolate, etc.

Elizabeth Connell

Chocolate Fridge Cake

Definitely not for dieting divas!

1 lb icing sugar
2 tablespoons cocoa
2 eggs, beaten
1 teaspoon vanilla
10 oz butter
1 packet Marie biscuits
4 oz walnuts

Sift together the icing sugar and cocoa. Slowly work in the eggs until the mixture is smooth. Add the vanilla. Melt the butter and add, working in well. Break the Marie biscuits roughly in quarters and fold in gently. Chop the walnuts coarsely and add. Turn the mixture out into 2 suitable cake tins or one long, shallow pie dish. Put into the fridge until firm and hard for about 4 hours. Serve as it is or with whipped cream.

Stuart Burrows

A Welsh lyric tenor who is best known for his interpretations of
Mozartian roles, particularly Idomeneo and Tamino. His
performances in *La Traviata*, *Eugene Onegin*, *Madama Butterfly*
and *La Damnation de Faust* and his frequent concert appearances
have also taken him all over the world.

Rich Fruit Cake

6 oz sultanas
6 oz currants
4 oz raisins
3 oz chopped mixed peel
3 oz glacé cherries
3 tablespoons sherry
4 oz butter
4 oz lard
7 oz dark brown sugar
4 large eggs
1 teaspoon vanilla essence

juice of half an orange
1 tablespoon black treacle, warmed
10 oz plain flour
1 teaspoon mixed spice
½ level teaspoon nutmeg
½ level teaspoon cinnamon
¼ level teaspoon cocoa
¼ level teaspoon coffee
a pinch of salt
2 oz ground almonds
2 oz chopped almonds

Pre-heat oven to Gas Mark 2 (300 °F, 150 °C).

Mix together all the fruit and soak in sherry overnight covered with a plate. On the following day, beat the fats together until soft. Add sugar and cream together until light and fluffy. Add eggs, one at a time, beating well after each egg. Add vanilla essence and orange juice. Stir in treacle and beat mixture again.

Sift flour, spices, cocoa, coffee and salt together and fold into creamed mixture. Stir in the ground almonds, soaked fruit and chopped almonds. Line a cake tin (8 inches square or 9 inches round) with greased greaseproof paper, and spoon in cake mixture. Spread to sides of tin leaving a slight dip in the centre so that the cake is even all over when rising. Tie a double layer of brown paper around the tin to prevent burning and rest a sheet of greased greaseproof paper on top of the brown paper.

Place cake at the centre of the oven at Gas Mark 2 for 1 hour. Reduce heat to Mark 1 (275 °F, 140 °C) for a further 2½ hours or until cooked. Test with a fine warmed steel knitting needle; the cake could take half an hour less or more because ovens vary. When cooked, leave cake in tin until cold then turn on to a wire tray, leaving greaseproof paper on cake until ready to use.

Valerie Masterson

Lazy Chocolate Cake

'A marvellous recipe because it keeps moist and can be decorated in many ways to tempt children and adults alike. It can also be used as a dessert cake with the addition of a little rum and served with cream.'

1 oz melted butter
4 oz flour
¼ teaspoon salt
1 teaspoon baking powder
8 oz sugar
2 eggs, beaten
2 fl oz milk
4 oz melted dark chocolate
1 teaspoon vanilla essence
1 teaspoon grated orange rind
orange juice
3 oz chopped hazelnuts

Icing
4 oz dark cooking chocolate
2 oz butter
1 tablespoon cornflour

Heat oven to 375 °F (Gas Mark 5). Grease a 7 inch cake tin with a teaspoon of the butter. Sift flour, salt and baking powder into a large bowl. Stir in sugar with wooden spoon. Make a well in the centre and pour in remaining butter, eggs and milk. Using the wooden spoon gradually incorporate the flour mixture with the liquids, stirring until you have a smooth batter. Stir in chocolate, vanilla essence, orange rind and juice beating until they are blended. Stir in nuts. Spoon mixture into cake tin, put in oven and bake for 35–40 minutes. Set aside to cool for 10 minutes. Remove from tin and place on wire rack.

To prepare the icing, melt chocolate in a heatproof mixing bowl over a saucepan of boiling water. Add butter and cornflour and beat until it forms a smooth paste. Remove from heat. With a flat-bladed knife, spread the icing all over the cake. Leave to cool for 30 minutes.

Gwynne Howell

Bran Biscuits

MAKES 20–24 BISCUITS

57 gm (2 oz) sugar
57 gm (2 oz) margarine
1 large egg
113 gm (4 oz) Prewett's 100% wholemeal plain flour
57 gm (2 oz) natural wheat bran
1 heaped teaspoon baking powder
pinch of salt

Cream sugar and margarine, beat in the egg, add other ingredients and knead into a dough. Roll out and cut into required shapes. Place on a prepared baking tray and bake for 20 minutes or until crisp and brown at 190 °C (375 °F, Gas Mark 5).

Janet Baker

Internationally well known, this English mezzo-soprano is
equally distinguished in opera, Lieder and concerts. Her
repertoire is enormous and she has sung in all major opera
houses, festivals and concerts throughout Europe, North and
South America and Great Britain. Much honoured, she was
awarded the CBE in 1970. She became a Dame Commander of
the British Empire in 1976. Among her many distinguished roles
are Hermia, Dido, Dorabella, Charlotte and Mary Stuart.

Ginger Biscuits

'If like me, you happen to be hooked on ginger biscuits, try
these – they are the best I've ever tasted. The trick is to roll them
thin so that they turn out crisp, and then to dunk them in coffee,
very quickly!'

MAKES 20–24 BISCUITS

½ lb margarine
1 lb self-raising flour
½ lb brown sugar
1 heaped dessertspoon ginger
½ lb golden syrup, warmed

Rub margarine into flour, add sugar, ginger and warmed syrup. Leave to set overnight. Place mixture on to a floured board and roll out very thinly. Cut into rounds using a 3 inch cutter. Place on a greased baking sheet and bake in a cool oven, Gas Mark 4, for 5 minutes until brown.

Marita Napier

Kourembiades (Cookies)

MAKES ABOUT 24 BISCUITS

1 lb butter
1 egg yolk
¾ cup powdered icing sugar
4½ cups (1 lb 11 oz) plain flour, sifted twice

Cream butter well, add egg yolk, mix well, add powdered sugar and blend. Slowly add flour and mix to a stiff batter. If it is too sticky to roll, chill for a short period. Roll into small balls, about ¾ inches in diameter. Bake on a baking sheet covered with greased greaseproof paper for 15–20 minutes at 350 °F. The cookies should stay pale. Cool and coat in powdered sugar.

Alberto Remedios

Shortbread

12 rounded tablespoons (12 oz) plain flour
2 rounded tablespoons (2 oz) cornflour
3 level tablespoons caster sugar
½lb butter

Mix the dry ingredients. Melt the butter and add to the dry ingredients. Spread in 2×7 inch flan tins and bake at 350 °F for 10 minutes. Lower to 300 °F for a further 30–45 minutes. Cut out into 6 or 8 squares or fingers while still warm.

Kiri te Kanawa

Maori Kisses

MAKES 6–8 KISSES

3 oz butter
3 oz caster sugar
4 oz flour
1 tablespoon cocoa
1 teaspoon cinnamon
1 teaspoon baking powder
6 oz dates

Butter Icing
3 oz icing sugar
1 oz butter
vanilla essence

Cream butter and sugar. Add dry ingredients and mix in dates. Shape into a flat round and cut into 6–8 pieces. Bake at 375 °F for 15 to 20 minutes. Cool. Ice with butter icing made by creaming the sugar and butter together with the vanilla essence.

Geraint Evans

Welsh Cakes

MAKES ABOUT 20 CAKES

1 lb flour
1 teaspoon baking powder
pinch salt
4 oz margarine
4 oz lard
4 oz currants
6 oz sugar
½ teaspoon mixed spice (optional)
1 egg
2 tablespoons milk

Sift the flour, baking powder and salt together. Rub in the fat and add the other dry ingredients. Beat the egg lightly and add with enough milk to make a firm paste. Roll out on a floured board to a thickness of ¼ inch and cut into rounds. Cook on a greased griddle for about 3 minutes on each side, until golden brown. Cool and sprinkle with sugar. Serve alone or with butter.

Eva Turner

King Haakin's Favourite Cakes

MAKES 10 CAKES

375 gm soft but not melted butter or margarine
500 gm plain flour
165 gm icing sugar
1 handful almonds (blanched and chopped)
1 egg

Rub the fat into the flour. Add icing sugar and then the almonds. Next, using the egg, make the mixture into a dough and roll into four 'sausages'. Leave in the refrigerator for a minimum of 2 hours.

Before cooking, cut rolls into slices about ⅛ inch thick and bake on a greased baking sheet for about 10 minutes at 200 °C (400 °F) near the top of the oven. The biscuits should be slightly pale brown at the edges when cooked.

Index of Recipes

Index of Contributors

The Opera House Cookbook